P9-AOX-333

Walt Disney Imagineering

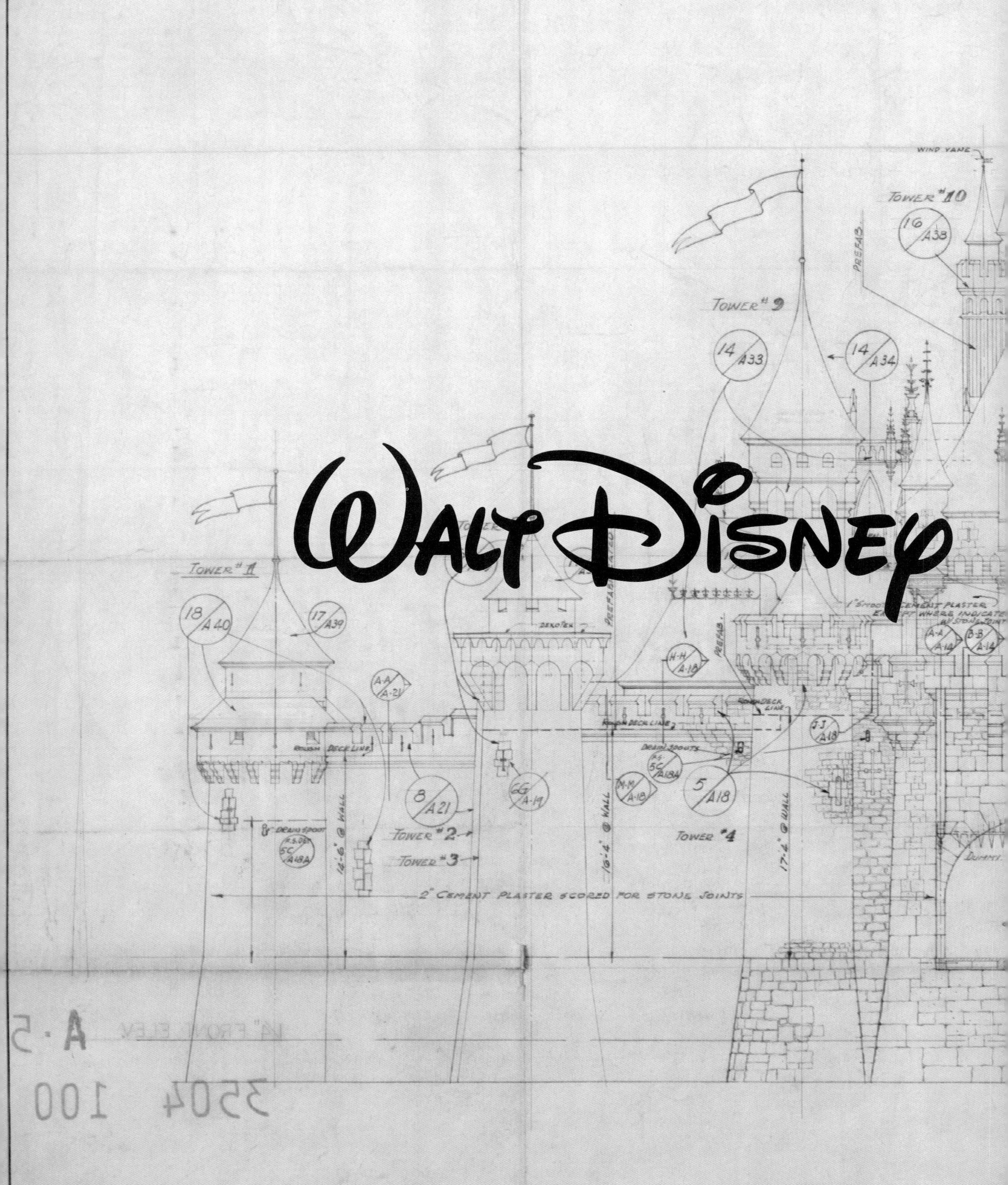

Walt Disney
WIND VANE
TOWER #10
16/A38
PREFAB.
TOWER #9
14/A33
14/A34
TOWER #11
18/A40
17/A39
PREFAB.
H-H/A-18
A-A/A-21
ROUGH DECK LINE
8/A21
6G/A-19
M-M/A-18
5/A18
J-J/A18
TOWER #2
TOWER #3
TOWER #4
12'-6" @ WALL
16'-4" @ WALL
17'-4" @ WALL
2" CEMENT PLASTER SCORED FOR STONE JOINTS
A-5

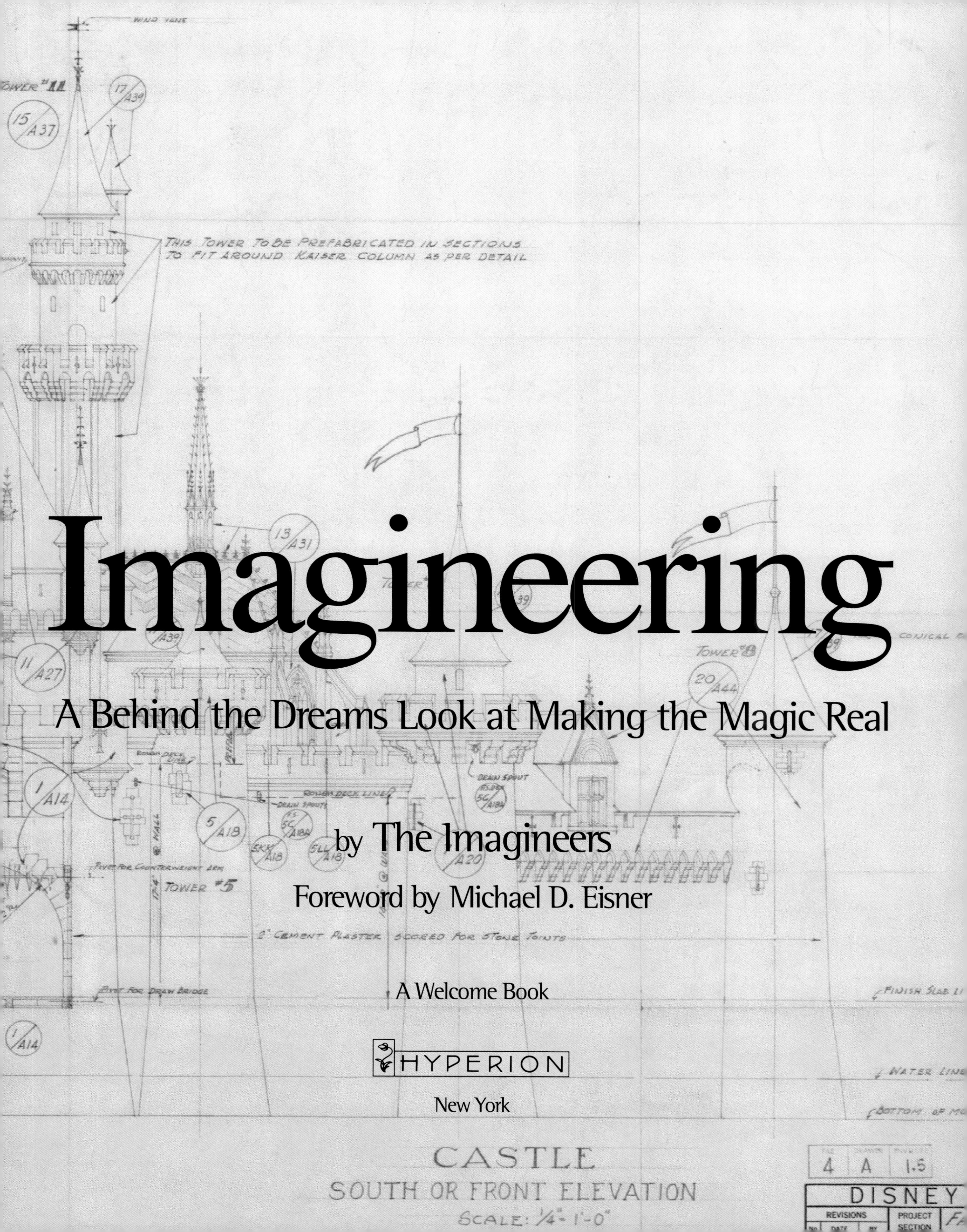

Imagineering

A Behind the Dreams Look at Making the Magic Real

by The Imagineers

Foreword by Michael D. Eisner

A Welcome Book

HYPERION

New York

ACKNOWLEDGMENTS

The Book Team wishes to thank:

Michael Eisner, Marty Sklar, Peter Rummell, and Ken Wong for their support of this project, Bob Miller for igniting the original spark, Wendy Lefkon and all the folks at Hyperion and Welcome for helping to turn our ideas into a real book.

Many thanks also to Pam Fisher, Melody Malmberg, Andy Sklar, Leticia Lelevier, and Scott Allen for helping us get the ball rolling, to Jim Hughey and Dave Thompson for helping make the business deal, and to Art Henderson, Matthew Priddy, Tom Fitzgerald, Michael Morris, and John Hench for their perspectives on Walt Disney Imagineering.

We would also like to thank Dave Smith, Robert Tieman, Sandra Sessler, Pam Young, Marlo Lee, Denise Brown, Mike Jusko, Diane Scoglio, Jill Centeno, Hugh Chitwood, Jess Allen, Michelle Kilbourne, Jan Oliver, Ernie Baily, David Katzman, Susan Mitchell, Bill Casey, Jack Gillett, Anne Tryba, Robbie Pallard, Kyle Barnes, Rudy Lord, Lizza Andres, Ed Squair, Saundra Murray, Danielle Burd, Chris Goosman, Kirk Winterroth, Bruce Vaughn, Marshall Monroe, and Earlene Paul for helping pull together the images and information that tell our story.

Written by Kevin Rafferty with Bruce Gordon
Image Selection and Research by Randy Webster and David Mumford

Copyright © 1996 Disney Enterprises, Inc.

Audio-Animatronics® is a registered trademark of The Walt Disney Company.

All rights reserved. No part of this book may be used or reproduced in any manner whatsoever without the written permission of the Publisher.

For information address:
Hyperion
114 Fifth Avenue
New York, New York 10011

Library of Congress Cataloging-in-Publication Data
Walt Disney imagineering : a behind the dreams look at making the magic real / by the Imagineers ; foreword by Michael D. Eisner.
p. cm.
ISBN 0-7868-6246-7
1. Walt Disney Company—Buildings—History. 2. Amusement parks—United States—Design—History. 3. Imagineers (Group)—History. I. Imagineers (Group) II. Walt Disney Company.
GV1851.W35 1996
725'. 76—dc20 96-9018
CIP

Produced by:
Welcome Enterprises, Inc.
575 Broadway
New York, New York 10012

Project Director: Hiro Clark
Hyperion Editor: Wendy Lefkon
Designer: Gregory Wakabayashi
Project Manager: Sara Baysinger

Printed and bound in Singapore
by Tien Wah Press

First Edition
10 9 8 7 6 5 4 3 2 1

CONTENTS

OPPOSITE: Communicating thoughts and ideas by "memo" is a major part of the Imagineering culture. An idea briefly explained in memo form can soon take on a life of its own, and one day might become a real project. For example, an inter-office envelope sent to Marty Sklar, Vice Chairman and Principal Creative Executive of Imagineering, contained the spark of an idea for this book. Marty got excited, and the result follows: the very first book all about Imagineering!

Walt Disney Imagineering

INTER-DEPARTMENTAL MAIL

NAME Marty Sklar
DEPARTMENT

NAME Kevin Rafferty
DEPARTMENT Show Writing

NAME Randy Webster
DEPARTMENT Collections Mgmt.

NAME David Mumford
DEPARTMENT SHOW SET DESIGN

NAME Bruce Gordon
DEPARTMENT Creative Development

NAME Jim Hughey
DEPARTMENT Finance

NAME DAVE S THOMPSON
DEPARTMENT FINANCE

NAME Christine Goosman
DEPARTMENT Show Writing

NAME Dan Young
DEPARTMENT COLLECTIONS MGMT.

NAME Mark Lee
DEPARTMENT CREATIVE SERVICES

NAME Denise Brown
DEPARTMENT Collections Mgmt.

NAME Mike Jusko
DEPARTMENT COLLECTIONS MGMT.

NAME Diane Scoglio
DEPARTMENT Creative Services

NAME JILL CENTENO
DEPARTMENT CREATIVE SERVICES

NAME Hugh Chitwood ☺
DEPARTMENT CREATIVE SERVICES

NAME Kirk Wintemroth
DEPARTMENT Program Management

Herbert Ryman

FOREWORD

Each time Imagineering and Hyperion approached me with the idea for this book, I thought to myself, "absolutely not." Naturally, being protective of everything Disney, I did not think it would be smart business to publish a book about Imagineering's "secret" process.

But the more I thought about it, the more I realized that even if the whole world knew exactly how Imagineering did what they did, no one could do exactly what the Imagineers can do. They are the best in the business. They invented the business. Imagineers are the only ones who can turn impossible dreams into real magic.

As I considered all of this, I was reminded of something Walt Disney once said:

> There's really no secret about our approach. We keep moving forward—opening new doors and doing new things—because we're curious. And curiosity keeps leading us down new paths. We're always exploring and experimenting . . . we call it Imagineering—the blending of creative imagination and technical know-how.

To Walt Disney's words, I must add that not only are the Imagineers curious, but they are courageous, outrageous, and their creativity is contagious.

And as far as blending creative imagination and technical know-how, they wrote the book on it—this book—about Imagineering by Imagineers, both past and present. However, it is not a book about the day-to-day "secret" operation of Walt Disney Imagineering as much as it is about what it feels like to be an Imagineer, to dream and to do.

Thanks to their dreams, themes, and magical schemes, the world is a happier place. Since the sun never sets on a Disney theme park, someone is smiling, laughing, singing, learning, caring, uniting, even forgetting about their most serious of worldly cares, even as you read these words. At this very moment, regardless of age, they are happily being swept away like a child in the magical embrace of a wondrous place created by those who build castles in the air as well as on the ground.

Michael D. Eisner
Chairman and CEO
The Walt Disney Company

ABOVE: Michael Eisner, Chairman and CEO, The Walt Disney Company.

OPPOSITE: Cinderella Castle towers above the entrance to Fantasyland in the Magic Kingdom at the Walt Disney World Resort, in this 1969 rendering by Herbert Ryman.

QUESTION: *How many Imagineers does it take to change a light bulb?*
ANSWER: *Does it have to be a light bulb?*

TO IMAGINEER

You won't find it in the dictionary. But any Imagineer can tell you the word is both a verb and a noun. To *imagineer.* To be an *Imagineer.* Like *Supercalifragilisticexpialidocious,* Imagineering has become a purely Disney word. The name combines imagination with engineering to describe both what we do and who we are. Creating a name for a group whose only job is to come up with ideas to build on—and then build those ideas—really took some Imagineering. But that is what Walt Disney was all about.

Walt seriously began to entertain the spark of an idea for a new kind of *themed* park in 1951 when he and movie art director, Harper Goff, began work on its first concept sketches. Soon afterwards, he hand-picked a small group of movie-makers from his studio, asking them to dedicate themselves to the design and development of this new and unique family fun park. Little did he know then that this small group would soon grow to become a major division of his company. But then again, maybe he did know.

Until this time, Walt knew little of the three-dimensional side of the entertainment fence, where fairs, amusement parks and the like could be found. But he did know movies and television. Driven by the desire to take his passion for storytelling far beyond the confines of two-dimensions, he landed on the idea that visitors who stepped in to this new park should feel as though they stepped into a movie. Every inch of the place should be part of a story, as in a movie or television show.

This is exactly why he enlisted the talents of a select handful of his studio people, setting them up in "secret" little offices around the lot. These were story people and visual people, animators, directors, writers, artists and set designers, a one-of-a-kind group who could set a scene and compose a breathtaking vista. These were the people who made the magic on Disney film. Now they were being asked to make the magic on Disney *land.* They began by making movies, but wound up making history.

They were the first Imagineers.

Standing firm upon the already established foundation of Disney values and optimism, this tiny team became the core of WED Enterprises (the initials stand for Walter Elias Disney), an independent company established in 1952 by Walt himself to help design and build his dream called Disneyland. Soon they all shared the dream. Combining their movie-making skills with a lot of learning, blood, sweat and tears, they eventually experienced firsthand what the watchers of their films came to believe: *the dream that you wish will come true.* In transforming a humble orange grove into a magic kingdom, they made movie magic real. And in doing so, they made real magic.

Walt and his first team of Imagineers invented the theme park business by inventing the process of "Imagineering." In the course of designing and building Disneyland, the process of "learning and succeeding by dreaming and doing" was employed for the very first time. These new Imagineers used their talents in ways they had never used them before to accomplish things they—or anyone else—had never accomplished before.

But that was only the beginning. There was still much work ahead. WED Enterprises soon moved from the Disney Studio in Burbank, California, to their own dedicated facility just down the street in the neighboring city of Glendale. Members of the first "handful" of Imagineers—including Ken Anderson, Roger Broggie, Bob Gurr, Bill Martin, John Hench, Bill Cottrell, Emile Kuri, Fred Joerger, Bill Evans, Sam McKim, Harriet Burns, Wathel Rogers, Dick Irvine, and Marvin Davis—stayed on with WED long after Disneyland was opened. Having experienced "Imagineering" together, they had become a family. Besides there was much work to do since Walt had made the promise that Disneyland would never be completed.

Since those early days, of course, much has been accomplished—and much has changed. Here at Imagineering, as with any dynamic group of people, the only constant we have is change.

After 1966, the Imagineers had to learn to carry on without the leadership of our greatest dreamer, when Walt Disney passed away on December 15th. Over the next two decades, inspired by the lessons Walt had taught us so well, we rallied together to reach new milestones with our most ambitious and successful projects yet, the Walt Disney World Resort, Tokyo Disneyland and Epcot Center.

In 1984, Michael Eisner and Frank Wells came on board to lead the Walt Disney Company, expanding the worlds of Disney in ways no one could have imagined (except perhaps the Imagineers, who can imagine anything!) Under the guidance of Michael and Frank, WED Enterprises became Walt Disney Imagineering. Though the name had changed, the mission would remain the same, and new milestones would continue to be reached.

In 1996, the tradition of change grew even stronger when Walt Disney Imagineering combined forces with Disney Development Company, the organization responsible for master planning and developing the dimensional worlds of Disney that lie *outside* the theme park borders. For the first time, this unique partnership would bring together the designers and the developers—the dreamers and the doers—working side by side to dream, design and build. Today, the primary responsibilities for carrying on the Imagineering tradition are in the hands of Peter Rummell, Chairman of Walt Disney Imagineering, Marty Sklar, Vice Chairman and Principal Creative Executive, and Ken Wong, President.

As you can imagine, an unparalleled spectrum of opportunity awaits. From the grandest plans for major attractions, hotels and whole new cities to the tiniest elements like light fixtures, restaurant menus, wallpaper and trashcans—every detail will be created by this combined team of Imagineers.

Countless worlds await, still unexplored.

Of course, for every spark of an idea we make real, there will always be hundreds that never get past a concept sketch, storyboard or model. Along the way, we have generated thousands upon thousands of original concept sketches, storyboard panels and paintings depicting each and every idea the Imagineers, including Walt, ever had.

At Imagineering, we have, in over four decades, accumulated more than 50,000 pieces of art that were created to help visualize the written or spoken words for all of these ideas. If we tried to put them all in one book, you'd need a coffee table the size of Epcot. So, we have selected the key pieces we feel best represent a sampling of projects we completed, came close to completing, or never completed at all.

Most of the illustrations and photographs we selected have never been seen outside our hallways. Therefore, we are about to "open the book" to share with you what has been imagined here for more than four decades.

Each and every image you see on the pages to follow, whether it represents a paper napkin sketch of a ride or an entire theme park, has one fundamental thing in common: It is the reason Imagineering came to be; it is why so many of our dreams have come true; it is why this book is in front of you right now.

It all begins with a spark.

OPPOSITE: Walt Disney—Dreamer and Doer.

"In the early days of Disneyland, it was incredible that WED accomplished all of the things it did because we were just a little machine shop and a tiny model shop. Of course, everything is bigger and better today, but I've never become blasé because I continue to have the feeling that Walt is looking over my shoulder."

—HARPER GOFF

These 1951 concept drawings by artist Harper Goff are among the first sketches depicting Walt Disney's idea for a little park celebrating America, which he planned to build across the street from the Disney studios. Harper based these Main Street drawings on Walt's boyhood memories of his hometown, Marceline, Missouri, as well as on memories of his own childhood home, Fort Collins, Colorado.

CLOCKWISE FROM THE TOP: Harper Goff's visions for the town's drug store and barbershop, the interior of the general store, and the town newspaper, *The Weekly Bugle*. The newspaper office was no doubt inspired by the days when a young Walt Disney earned money for his family by selling newspapers in Kansas City. The general store would become a featured part of Main Street when Disneyland opened in 1955. And on Opening Day, Disneyland also had its own 1890's-style newspaper, *The Disneyland News*. Its editor, Marty Sklar, is now Vice Chairman of Imagineering.

"One of our first ideas for Main Street was a corset shop called 'The Wizard of Bras.' For some reason, Walt didn't like it."

–BILL MARTIN

ABOVE: **As Walt Disney's ideas for his proposed park continued to grow, he asked Harper Goff to lay them out in this first bird's-eye view of the eleven-acre Riverside Drive property located directly across the street from the studio, the site where Walt hoped to build his park.**

"I could never convince the financiers that Disneyland was feasible because dreams offer too little collateral."

—WALT DISNEY

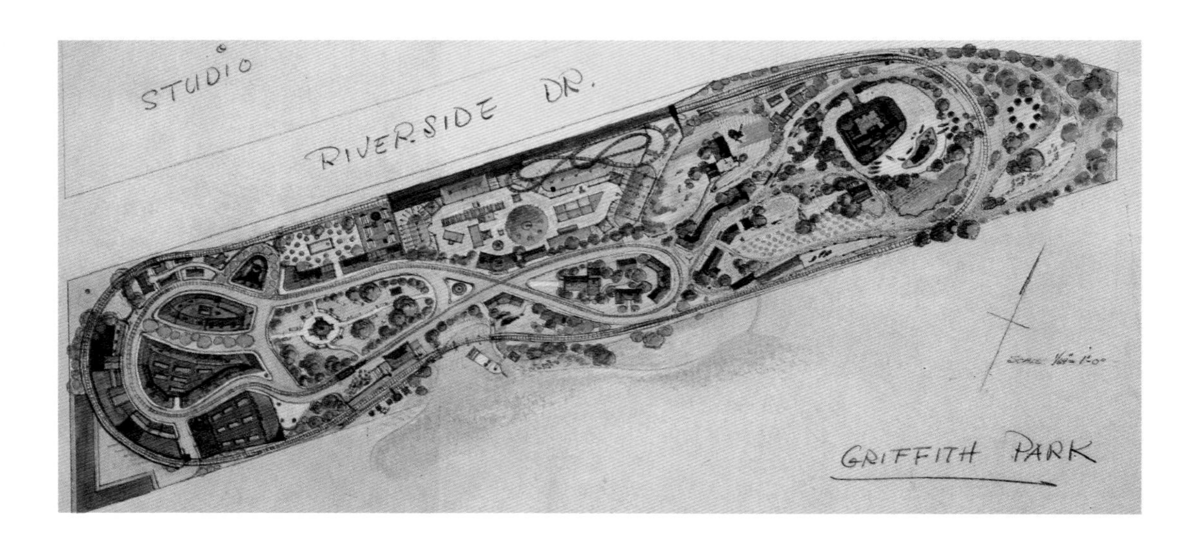

RIGHT: **Harper Goff created this aerial view site plan, which shows how the differently themed areas and the rapidly developing attraction ideas might fit together. The headquarters building for Walt Disney Feature Animation, completed in 1994, exists on this very site today.**

LEFT: **As ideas for the park grew, so too its size. In this plan, Harper Goff pushed the Riverside Drive site all the way out to its sixteen-acre limit. It soon became apparent that this site would not be large enough to accommodate all the things Walt and the first Imagineers were dreaming, so the search began for a new piece of property. Today, the Ventura Freeway, which runs parallel to Riverside Drive, cuts through the middle of the site.**

"We had to take on things we never dreamed we'd have to take on."

—FRED JOERGER

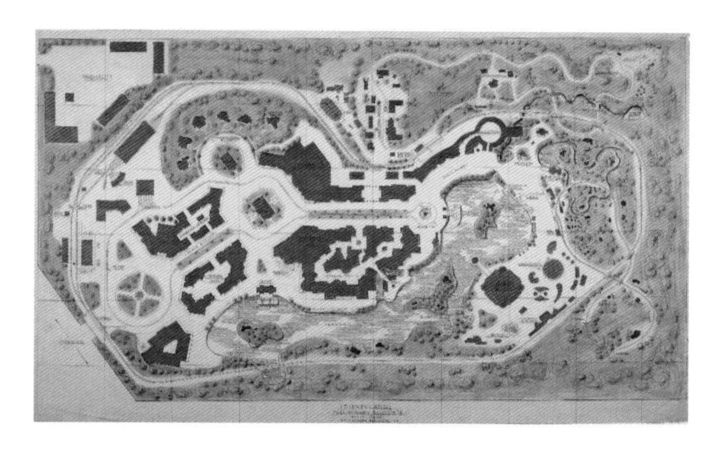

ABOVE: After Walt Disney questioned the Imagineers as to what they might do with fifty acres of land for the park, art director Marvin Davis attempted to fit everything they had designed thus far onto this site plan—three times the size of Riverside Drive. At the time of this drawing, the actual site for Disneyland had yet to be determined. Each square section of the grid represents one square acre of land.

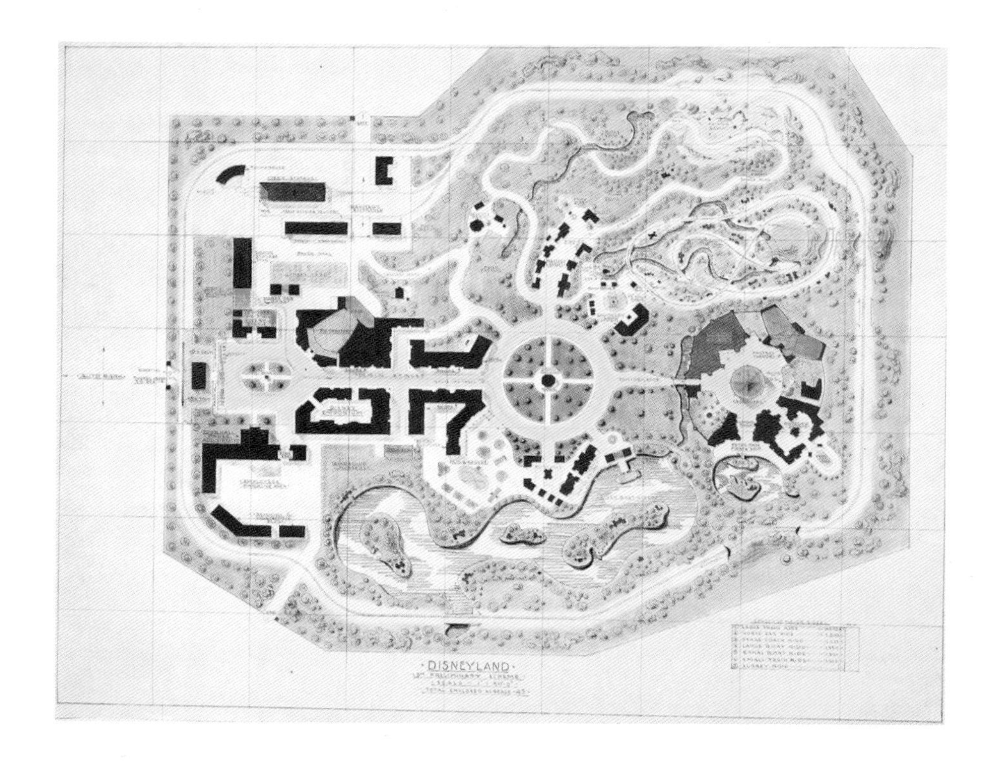

ABOVE RIGHT: Marvin Davis created the first site plan to include the "central hub" concept, in which differently themed lands would surround a center point in the park. From this hub, guests would have the opportunity to step into the land of their choice.

"The year was 1953. Walt said, 'Hi, Herbie. I'm over here at the Studio. I wonder if you could come over here. Just come the way you are, I'll be out front waiting for you.' I was curious, and flattered that he picked up the phone and called me. I had no idea what he wanted. He met me out front and shook my hand saying, 'Hi Herbie, we're in the Zorro Building.' So we went in, and I asked what this was all about. He said, 'Well, we're going to do an amusement park.' I said, 'That's good and exciting. So what do you want to see me about?' He said, 'My brother Roy has to go to New York on Monday morning. He's got to talk to some bankers there. You know bankers don't have any imagination, none at all. You have to show them what you're going to do. Roy has to show them what this place is going to look like.' And I said, 'Well, I'd like to see what this place is going to look like, too. Where have you got all this stuff?' I thought maybe it was in the other room. Walt said, 'You're going to do it.' I said, 'No I'm not.' There was a brief pause. Walt paced back and forth—we were alone in the room. He went over to the corner and he turned his head around with his back to me and said, 'Will you do it if I stay here with you?' 'Yes, I'll do it if you stay here.'"

—HERBERT RYMAN

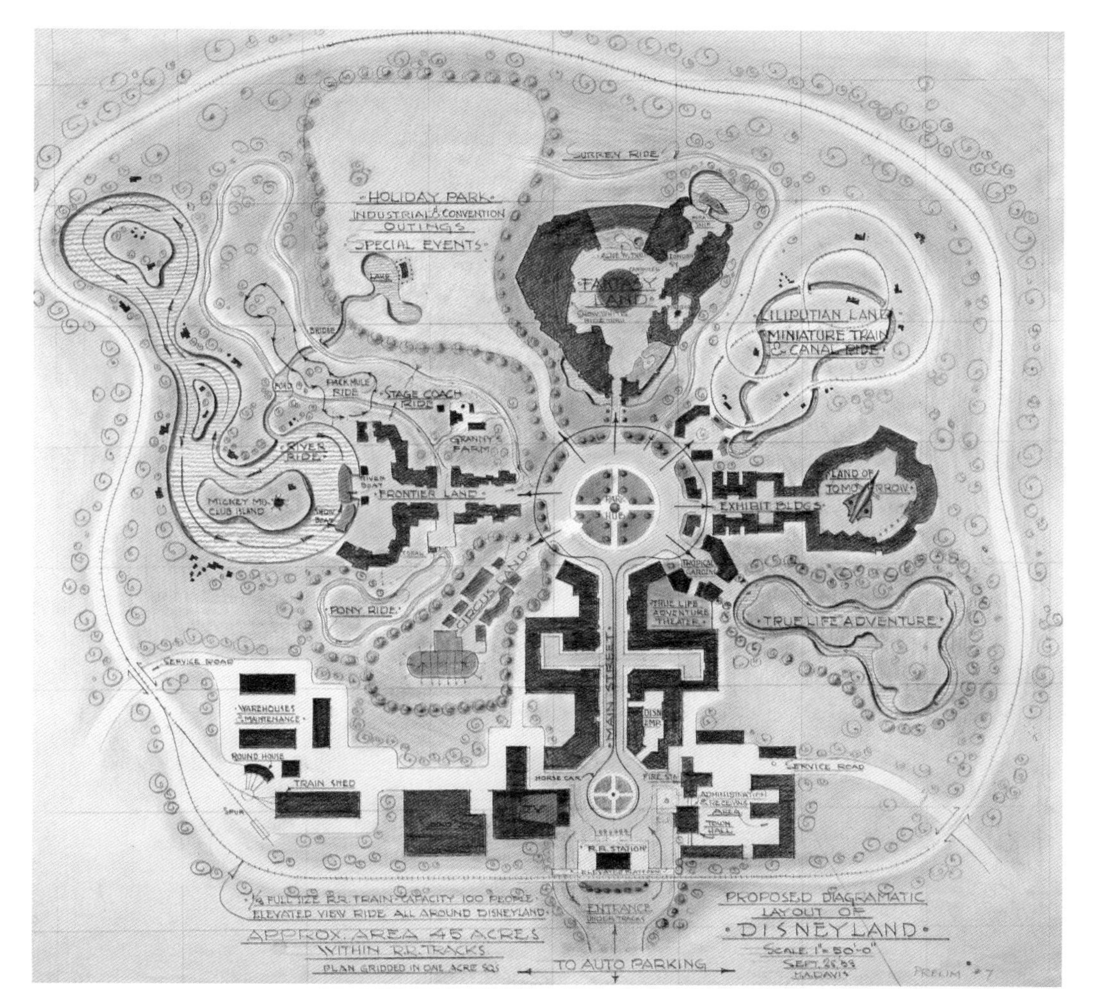

LEFT: Once Marvin Davis had created a series of detailed building elevations, he created a second-generation "hub" plan to see how it would all come together. This was the plan used by Walt Disney and Herbert Ryman as a practical reference for the creation of the first bird's-eye view of Disneyland.

OVERLEAF: In September, 1953, Walt spent one entire weekend with Herbert Ryman, art director for such films as *Fantasia*, *Dumbo*, and *Pinocchio*. They completed this first-ever bird's-eye view of Disneyland in two days.

DISNEYLAND
OPERA HOUSE
DISNEYLAND
DISNEYLAND
SCHEMATIC AERIAL VIEW
APPROX. 45 ACRES
WITHIN RAILROAD TRACKS
DESIGNED BY WED ENTERPRISES

"Herbie, I just want it to look like nothing else in the world. And it should be surrounded by a train."

—WALT DISNEY

"All I want you to think about is when people walk through or have access to anything you design, I want them, when they leave, to have smiles on their faces. Just remember that. It's all I ask of you as a designer."

—WALT DISNEY

ABOVE: **Since this painting would be used for the public unveiling of Disneyland, Walt Disney asked special effects matte painter Peter Ellenshaw to paint it in the form of a large, realistic rendition. Since there was no canvas available large enough to accommodate the size he had in mind, Peter went to the animation department to permanently borrow one of their well-used 40" x 90" storyboards. Over the years, the animators had used push-pins to mount countless story sketches on the board, so before Peter could even get started with his painting he was faced with the daunting task of having to fill in the hundreds of push-pin holes with a thick coat of paint.**

TOP: **Walt posed with Peter Ellenshaw's dramatic rendering of Disneyland. It was the piece of artwork which introduced the concepts for the park to the world on Walt's weekly television series, *Disneyland*, on October 27, 1954.**

"I caught sight of a man far down the street. Alone. Quietly regarding the place he had so long envisaged, now complete, ready to bring pleasure and happy satisfactions to the millions who will visit it. And I was reminded that he, too, was a Main Streeter, never weaned away from the common bond with the great majority of American small town and country folk, their tastes and ideals, despite long identification with big cities as an eminent world figure."

—JACK JUNGMEYER
The Disneyland News, July 1955

NOT CHILD ENOUGH

Dear sirs: I think it goes without saying that I am as critical as you people are of many facets of American life. Lord knows I've raised my voice often enough. But when someone like Julian Halevy equates Disneyland and Las Vegas (The Nation, June 7), I begin to doubt his or my sanity.

Not that I haven't met his type before. The world is full of people who, for intellectual reasons, steadfastly refuse to let go and enjoy themselves. Mr. Halevy damns himself immediately when he states he is glad he didn't take a child with him to Disneyland. I did better than take a child; my first visit, I accompanied one of the great theatrical and creative minds of our time, Charles Laughton. I've never had such a day full of zest and good humor. Mr. Laughton is no easy mark; he has a gimlet eye and a searching mind. Yet he saw, and I found, in Disneyland, vast reserves of imagination before untapped in our country.

I admit I approached Disneyland with many intellectual reservations, myself, but these have been banished in my seven visits. Disney makes mistakes; what artist doesn't? But when he flies, he really flies. I shall be indebted to him for a lifetime for his ability to let me fly over midnight London looking down on that fabulous city, in his Peter Pan ride. The Jungle Boat ride, too, is an experience of true delight and wonder. I could go on, but why bother?

I have a sneaking suspicion, after all is said and done, that Mr. Halevy truly loved Disneyland but is not man enough, or child enough, to admit it. I feel sorry for him. He will never travel in space, he will never touch the stars.

—RAY BRADBURY

From *Letters to the Editor, NATION*, June 28, 1958

ABOVE: The very same Peter Ellenshaw painting, this time illuminated under ultraviolet blacklight which transforms the painting into a dramatic nighttime scene. Calling on his special effects background, Peter treated all the streetlights, windows and illuminated signs in his rendering with a special paint that glows under blacklight. This same kind of paint has been used ever since to magically illuminate the scenes in many Disney attractions.

RIGHT: Taken that first summer in 1955, this aerial photograph demonstrates how accurately Peter Ellenshaw's painting—completed before groundbreaking—illustrated the future layout of the park. It is a tribute to Walt's vision to note how many of the early concepts actually became part of the "dream come true."

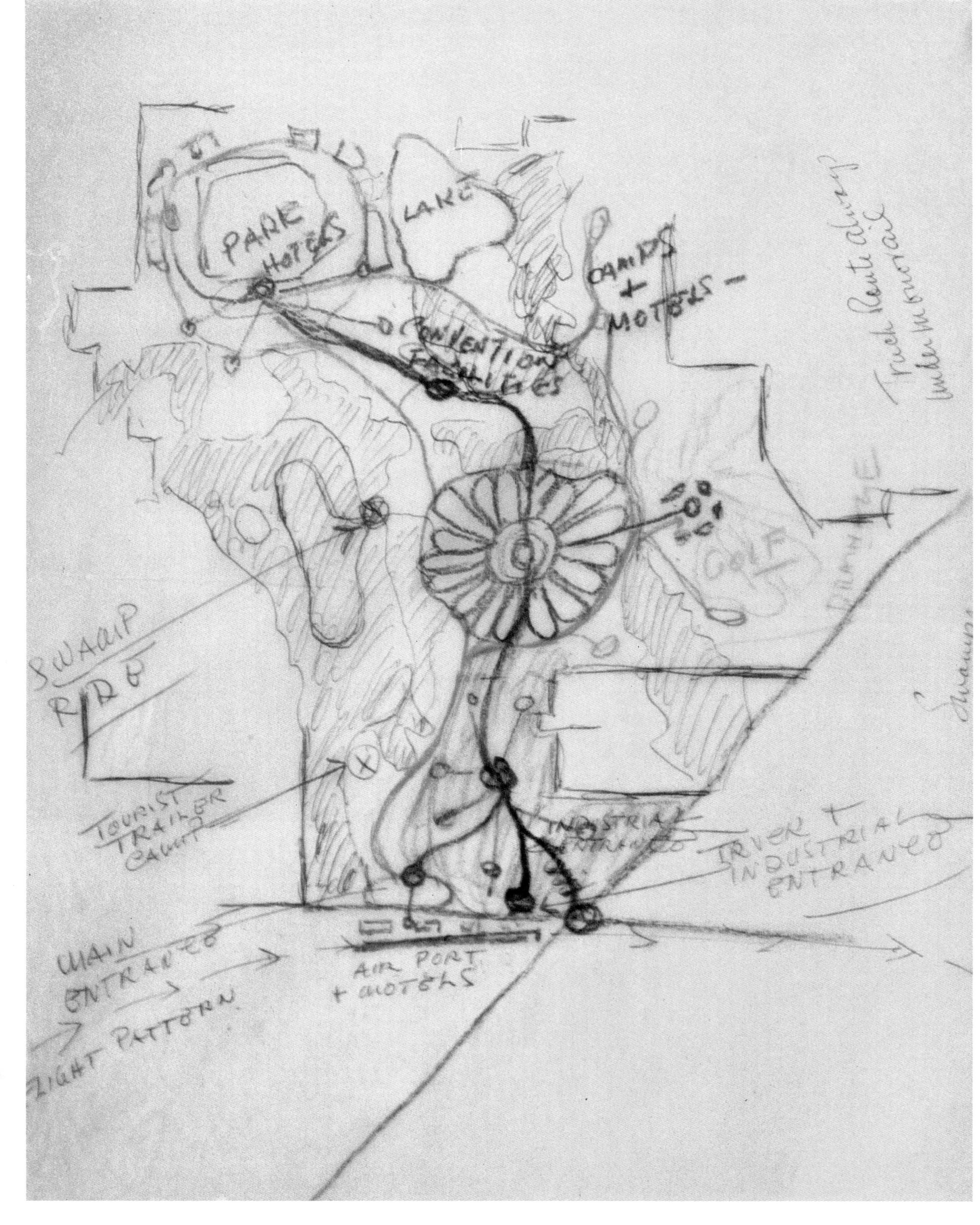

PARK
HOTELS
LAKE
CAMPS
+
MOTELS
CONVENTION
FACILITIES
GOLF
SWAMP
TOURIST
TRAILER
CAMP
INDUSTRIAL
ENTRANCE
RIVER +
INDUSTRIAL
ENTRANCE
MAIN
ENTRANCE
FLIGHT PATTERN
AIR PORT
+ MOTELS

CHAPTER 1

THE SPARK

A raging fire begins with a mere spark. Around Imagineering, the spark of an idea ignites, gains momentum, and consumes us in everything we do. The tiniest spark of an idea is no small thing. Even if born upon the tattered edge of a paper napkin, it may very well grow up to be the size of something special. Each and every spark gets its chance. Here, *what if* actually means *why not*. "Everyone starts with a blank sheet of paper," says Marty Sklar, President of Imagineering. "There are two ways to look at a blank sheet of paper. You can look at it as the most frightening thing in the world, or as the greatest opportunity in the world because nobody's put anything on it. That's the way we look at it around here. You can dream, create new things, and let your imagination go. No one's going to stomp on you because you came up with a strange, weird idea, because that's what your leaders expect from you."

At Imagineering, a blank sheet of paper can exist in the form of a napkin from lunch, a canvas, a block of foam, a lump of clay, a scrap of wood, or an entire wall. The initial idea flows from the brain to the hand and onto the paper in the form of words and/or images.

These ideas are then shared with a handful of Imagineers who gather to bounce them around. We call this brainstorming (a.k.a. contagious enthusiasm). Usually, when a brainstorming session begins, there are no certainties. To us that simply means anything is possible.

Quick thumbnail sketches and other thoughts inspired by the original spark are put down on scratch paper and note cards. Many are done in jest, while others get right to the heart of the matter. Realistic or far-fetched, each contribution is an important part of the process—they all help mold, shape, and improve the idea. A brainstorming may last hours, days, even weeks. (If donuts are included, we may stretch it out a while longer.) The only rule during this time: there are no rules.

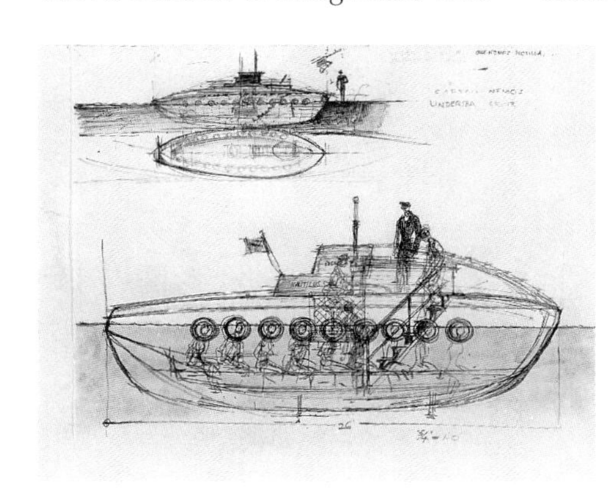

As Imagineers dream and scheme, things can get serious or silly, frustrating or fun. Each idea is approached with minds open to any intriguing possibility. Every aspect is questioned, admired, debated, and turned upside down and inside out until that first sketch can take a daring leap off the napkin and grow into larger, more defined drawings and paintings. The brainstorming subsides when the basic idea is defined, understood, and agreed upon by all group members. It belongs to all of us, keeping strong a rich heritage left to us by Walt Disney. Teamwork is truly the heart of Imagineering.

In that spirit, though Imagineering is a diverse collection of architects, engineers, artists, support staff members, writers, researchers, custodians, schedulers, estimators, machinists, financiers, model-makers, landscape designers, special effects and lighting designers, sound technicians, producers, carpenters, accountants, and filmmakers—we all have the honor of sharing the same unique title. Here, you will find only *Imagineers*.

Oh, and plenty of blank paper.

ABOVE: John Hench created this concept sketch in 1964 to depict a new thrill attraction known as Space Port, intended for Tomorrowland at Disneyland. The attraction came to be known as Space Mountain.

BELOW LEFT: This anonymous sketch of an underwater submarine voyage is among the earliest created—a surprisingly accurate prediction of the actual submarines that began operation in Disneyland in 1959.

OPPOSITE: Walt Disney drew this sketch in 1966 to illustrate how the recently acquired Florida property should be laid out. The flower petal shape in the center of the sketch represents Epcot, which would come to be known as Walt's greatest dream. When Walt Disney World opened in 1971, five years after Walt's death, the Magic Kingdom was built at the furthest edge of the property, exactly where he had placed it. A decade later, Epcot Center opened on the very site of his future city.

The tiniest spark of an idea is no small thing. Even if born upon the tattered edge of a paper napkin, it may very well grow up to be the size of something special.

ABOVE: Walt Disney asked Herbert Ryman to draw up some sketches that would capture the romance of New Orleans. The Royal Court, seen here, would become a central focus of New Orleans Square when it opened at Disneyland in 1966. The stairway in the center of the sketch leads to a suite of rooms that would have been a private apartment for Walt Disney. (Walt passed away before the apartment was ever used.) Today, the rooms are part of The Disneyland Gallery.

TOP: In 1992, industrial designer Bill Casey proposed this concept for a 1930s streamline-style train as a solution for transporting guests from a planned remote parking area to the main entrance of The Disneyland Resort.

ABOVE: The Typhoon Lagoon concept team members sketched potential typhoon-inspired story themes. Among them were a lost temple uncovered, a water-logged logging camp and a beached cruise ship. Randy Bright, then creative executive, was immediately drawn to this sketch by Chris Runco. The park would be filled with objects from faraway places that had been blown in by a freak storm. Guests who look closely at "Miss Tilly"'s stern sitting high atop the mountain may be surprised to discover that her home port is "Safen Sound, Fla.".

ABOVE: In 1978, Herbert Ryman created this early rendering of Epcot Center, one of the first to show the park's landmark geodesic sphere, Spaceship Earth. Designer John Hench saw the opening of his conception in 1982 as the world's largest free-standing geosphere.

BELOW: An early concept for The Land pavilion at Epcot by designer Tony Baxter featured giant glass "biomes," each one representing a different climate zone, from hot dry deserts to humid jungles and icy polar caps. Walking tours, giant hot-air balloons and subterranean tunneling machines would allow guests to experience the wonders found on, above and below The Land.

RIGHT: This thumbnail sketch by concept architect Chris Carradine was the first image to evolve from a brainstorm session for the project that was to become Pleasure Island at Walt Disney World. This rough sketch contained the visual information necessary to define the place the team was trying to conceptualize.

BELOW RIGHT: Walt Disney sparked his Imagineers to sketch ideas for a Matterhorn mountain attraction at Disneyland, which opened in 1959. Twenty-five years later, designer Claude Coats created this sketch of the Matterhorn for a proposed Switzerland pavilion in World Showcase at Epcot.

ABOVE: Herbert Ryman often made preliminary sketches to familiarize himself with the subject matter—in this case Tokyo Disneyland. This drawing demonstrates his sense for shapes, forms and the surrounding environment.

RIGHT: This early inspirational sketch by Andy Sklar begins to define the concept of Innoventions, an Epcot showcase of current and future technologies and lifestyles. Drawings and paintings building on this one helped the Imagineers convey the Innoventions concept to the many international companies whose products and displays would be presented as part of the show.

While conceptualizing, our thoughts are unrestrained. Limitations only weigh on the wings of an idea as it soars wild and free on the updrafts of possibility. Creative freedom allows us to do anything imaginable, anything at all.

ABOVE: **Bringing inanimate characters to life and giving them distinct personalities were the challenges answered in the concept sketch for Roger Rabbit's Car Toon Spin, created in 1991 by artist Marcelo Vignali.**

TOP: **The moment a spark ignites, Imagineers gather in brainstorming sessions. Here, Imagineering Vice Chairman Marty Sklar (center) confers with (from left) Joe Lanzisero, Kevin Rafferty, Mel Malmberg and Steve Kirk.**

LEFT: **In creating this children's play space for the Disney Cruise Lines, Joe Lanzisero and Dave Minichiello were sensitive to the limited amount of space available on deck. As suggested in this concept rendering by Dave, the space was designed to serve many functions. Besides providing a costume room in the hull for high seas role playing, and play equipment themed as a ship's cargo for daytime activities, the "galleon" includes a multi-purpose stage to accommodate live performances and Disney classic films by night. Not pictured but above the deck are fiber-optic constellations that sparkle in the shape of Disney characters.**

Snow Such Thing as a Bad Idea

At Walt Disney Imagineering, there is no such thing as a bad idea. Each idea initially exists in a blue sky phase where we are free to test, experiment, and imagine with the hope and intent that we will get somewhere. Sometimes ideas come from left field, while other times they fulfill a need. The latter was the case when we came up with the idea for the Blizzard Beach Water Adventure Park, at Walt Disney World.

Imagineering was asked to create another themed water park—our Typhoon Lagoon was so successful that hundreds of visitors were turned away each day. A small team of Imagineers, led by Senior Vice Presidents Eric Jacobson and Kathy Mangum, brainstormed ideas for a new park.

Eric's office is filled with lots of strange and unusual objects. He is most proud, however, of his vast collection of snow domes. "Too bad," Eric said as he shook one of the domes to make the snow flurry inside, "we can't make a park out of one of these." "Why not?" responded Marshall Monroe, who suddenly sparked the crazy idea for a snowy ski resort in sunny central Florida. Jokingly, artist Tim Kirk sketched a crazed, ear-muffed alligator swishing down a slope on skis, while artist Julie Svendsen, with tongue in cheek, rendered the ski resort as it would appear inside a snow dome. As outrageous as it seemed, the idea proved irresistible.

Constructing an entire water park inside a giant snow dome was out of the question. So the team created a legend that a freak winter storm blew through central Florida, stopping just long enough to dump a mountain of snow on the area's highest hill, thus prompting the construction of the state's first-ever ski resort.

As the legend goes, the hot tropical sun returned and quickly melted all the snow. The ski runs turned to water, and the run-off created some of the tallest, fastest, and wildest water slides found anywhere in the world. So instead of skis, poles, and jackets, "skiers" at this resort come equipped with bathing suits, towels, and suntan lotion.

Thanks to a simple snow dome, the concept for a 43-acre water adventure park was born, which just goes to show—every good idea deserves a fair shake.

"We call them gag sessions. We get in there and toss ideas around. And we throw them in and put all the minds together and come up with something and say a little prayer and open it and hope it will go."

—WALT DISNEY

ABOVE: The overall theme for Blizzard Beach was inspired by a little snow dome in Imagineer Eric Jacobson's office. This was the first sketch to emerge after the brainstorm shifted into a blizzard—proof that a simple image can communicate a theme and set a major design process in motion.

TOP: This coldsnap-happy fellow, sketched by designer Tim Kirk, would eventually ski himself to fame as Ice Gator, the official mascot of Blizzard Beach.

RIGHT: Brainstorming sessions produced a blizzard of Blizzard Beach ideas. Concepts for everything from attractions and characters to costumes, names and gags are gathered together on idea boards like this one.

A blank piece of paper becomes our launching pad. It is a window that opens wide to the sky, inviting our idea to take off and fly!

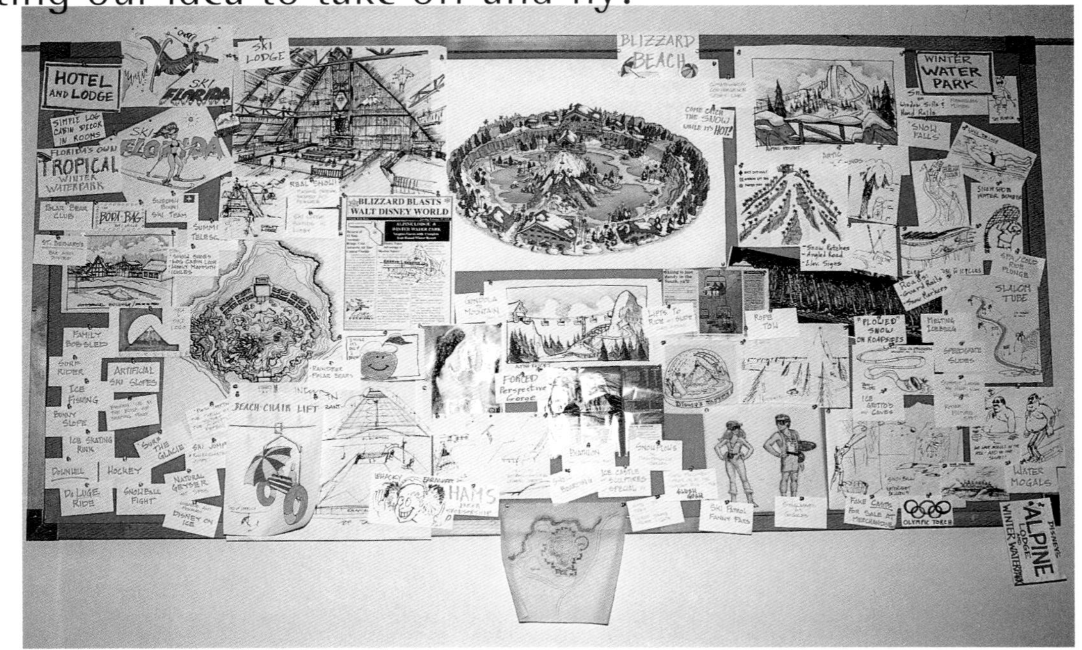

ABOVE: This concept sketch by Marcelo Vignali shows the wonderful time that will be had by all at Blizzard Beach, especially this sweltering (and rapidly melting) family, anxious to chill out in the refreshing coolness of Blizzard Beach.

LEFT: The purpose of this Tim Kirk sketch was to explore how the architecture of a typical ski resort could lend itself to a sunny Florida location. The comical contrast between hot and cold established the tropical alpine style that served as the design model for the entire park. Versions of the elements suggested in this sketch can be found in the park today.

BELOW: In keeping with the overriding theme of Blizzard Beach, the design team suggested that a snow blower be customized to pour a steady flow of chilled water into the warm waters of Cross Country Creek. Richard Vaughn sketched up the idea, it was approved—and built!

"Build this? Are you kidding? Sure we can build this!"

—KATHY MANGUM

"We had three or four other concepts, but we kept coming back to the ski resort theme. It just seemed perfect to mix up all the metaphors we have for skiing and going to the beach: hot and cold, snow and sand, ice and water. This is one ski resort where you won't break a leg."

—ERIC JACOBSON

"If I could pick any job here, I'd move my office to the Imagineering building and immerse myself in all that lunacy and free-thinking."

—MICHAEL D. EISNER
Wall St. Journal, Jan. 6, 1987

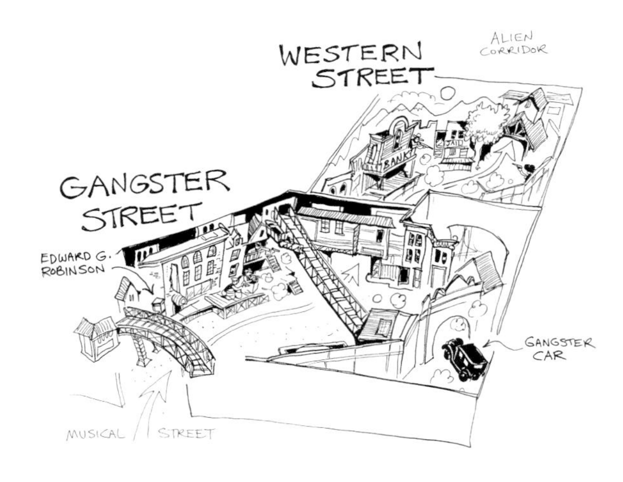

TOP: The Great Movie Ride, originally envisioned as an attraction at Epcot, is seen here in its proposed location, nestled between Journey into Imagination (left) and The Land (right).

ABOVE: Tim Kirk created this early concept sketch showing how scenes inside the Great Movie Ride might be portrayed.

THE GREAT MOVIE RIDE IDEA

An idea can change tremendously during its development. Even though a story theme may remain true to its original spark to opening day, its physical design may experience hundreds, if not thousands, of alterations.

Not long after Michael Eisner became Chief Executive Officer of The Walt Disney Company, he began to spend a lot of time at Imagineering "immersing [himself] in all the lunacy and free thinking." Being an idea man himself (not to mention a big kid at heart), he fit right in. Among the first concepts he encountered was an idea sparked by Marty Sklar and Randy Bright (then Imagineering creative executives) for a Hollywood studio-themed "entertainment pavilion" at Epcot. The concept featured a ride that would take guests on a journey into the magic of the movies—literally.

As a team of Imagineers began to develop the ride concept, its rich theme prompted several offshoot ideas. It soon became apparent to Michael that this "great movie ride" concept should be expanded in its design to a scale even more grand than an Epcot pavilion.

The Imagineers came up with a solution, and The Great Movie Ride was indeed built—surrounded by the 45-acre Disney-MGM Studios!

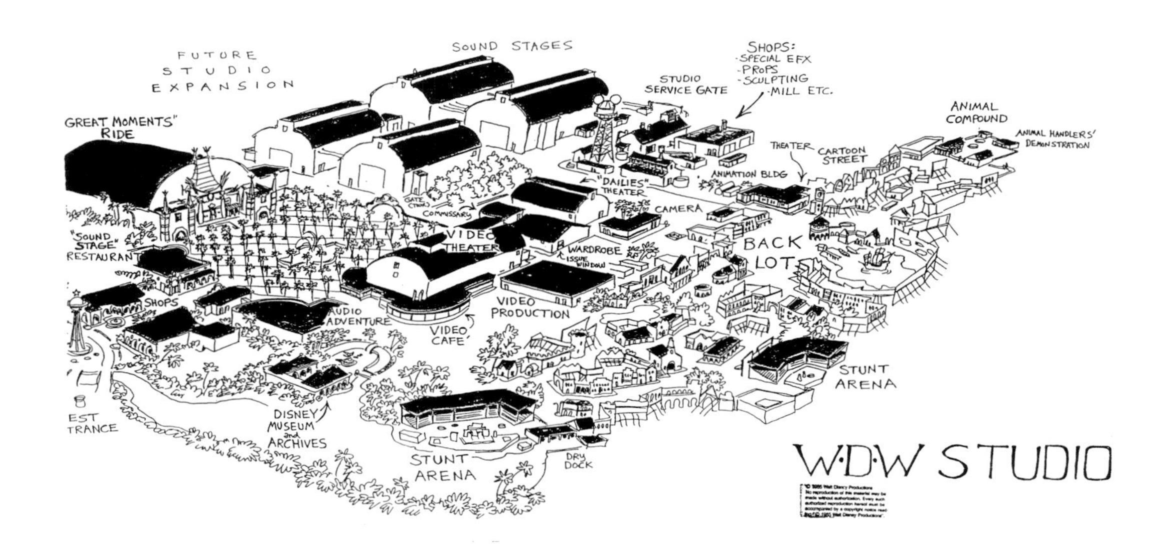

ABOVE: Collin Campbell created this dramatic night-time view of Hollywood Boulevard, the Main Street of the Studio.

LEFT: Tim Kirk drew this very first sketch of what the Disney-MGM Studios might look like—and the finished park is almost exactly the way Tim envisioned it.

ABOVE: In 1960, the Ford Motor Company asked Walt Disney to create a unique show for the 1964-1965 New York World's Fair. John Hench created this sketch of what the pavilion might look like, including the dramatic exterior tubes of the Magic Skyway. Ford wanted guests to ride along the skyway inside real Ford convertibles—that would be automatically piloted and capable of traveling through the entire show inside and outside the pavilion. The result was a revolutionary Disney-designed ride system that steered the vehicles like giant slot cars, with powerful drive wheels pushing against the bottom of the cars to propel them along the track. Variations of this ride system would forever change the face of theme parks, and allowed the development of attractions ranging from the PeopleMover at Disneyland to Spaceship Earth at Epcot.

BELOW: Progressland, the General Electric pavilion at the New York World's Fair, as envisioned by artist Claude Coats in this 1963 rendering. The dome of the theater was covered with thousands of animated colored lights whose motion (designed by General Electric) made it appear that the whole building was revolving, in honor of its featured show, "Walt Disney's Carousel of Progress."

"Walt Disney Imagineering is a true Renaissance organization. The only people I see who are successful at changing the world are right here—people with very special dreams."

—RAY BRADBURY

A FAIR CHALLENGE

Could the magic of Disneyland live outside the park? That was the question Robert Moses, organizer of the 1964-1965 New York World's Fair, asked Walt as plans got underway for the fair.

Walt was extremely excited about the opportunity to discover whether there was an outside market for the Disneyland experience. He was equally excited to find a proving ground on which to test WED's newly-developed entertainment designs and technologies, including ride systems and human Audio-Animatronics figures.

Though uncertain about the practical use of WED's unrefined show technologies, Walt convinced the sponsors of the proposed shows—the Pepsi-Cola Company, Ford Motor Company, the State of Illinois and General Electric—that he could entertain while educating hundreds of thousands of fairgoers. True to his word, Walt and the Imagineers produced four of the most popular shows at the New York World's Fair.

With 91% of fairgoers enjoying at least one of the four Disney shows, the question of whether the magic of Disneyland could exist outside the berm was answered. The fact that the Disney shows proved to be so popular at the fair was a prime factor in the decision to proceed with a new project called Walt Disney World.

RIGHT: Walt felt that It's a Small World needed to have a dramatic landmark of its own, and asked designer Rolly Crump—legendary within Imagineering for his fanciful sculptures and mobiles—to create a giant tower that would provide the colorful kinetics Walt envisioned. Rolly's solution is seen in this sketch by Paul Hartley of the Tower of the Four Winds, a magical, ever-turning mobile which graced the outside of the pavilion for the two years of the fair. Sadly, there was no budget available to save the tower after the fair closed.

BELOW: Walt Disney challenged his Imagineers to create a dignified animated figure of Abraham Lincoln for the New York World's Fair, as envisioned in this sketch by Sam McKim. The Imagineers estimated the project would take at least five years—but managed to make it happen in half that time, ready for the opening of the fair in 1964.

OVERLEAF: Inside the Wonder Rotunda, guests would ride in real Ford convertibles on a journey along the Magic Skyway that began in the days of the dinosaurs and ended sometime in the future. In this rendering by Sam McKim, lucky visitors are launched into the world of tomorrow's transportation.

Only when we curiously observe the spark from our many different perspectives, thus creating new ideas to enhance the original, does it burst into illuminating flame.

ABOVE: Ideas and discoveries derived from the development of a proposed Burbank Entertainment Center, seen here in a sketch by Bill Block from a design by Chris Carradine, assisted in the further evolution of Pleasure Island at the Walt Disney World Resort.

EXTINGUISHING A SPARK

New ideas are continuously nourished as long as they have a shot at reality. The process of developing an idea can be temporarily stopped at any time for many reasons, including change in concept direction, a change in project priority, or even a change of mind. If there is no longer a need or a place for a project as *designed,* it will be discontinued regardless of how fantastic it might be. This difficult but necessary turn of events can occur during any stage of its development.

Though the spark for a project may have been snuffed out, much is learned from all ideas, no matter how short-lived they might be. New technologies initially developed for a canceled project can prove to be just what we need for a future idea.

Today, there are several fully developed but dormant concepts on the shelves at Imagineering. They are not dust collectors. They are among our most valued assets. Many are stored on the lower shelves so they can be easily uncovered time and again for research or inspiration. As for those way up on top—you should have seen the ones that got away.

ABOVE: Artist Bill Justice created this sketch for a proposed Dumbo's Circus attraction at Disneyland, envisioned for a site in Fantasyland near Storybook Land. Though the Circus was never built, the site did become the home of Videopolis, which opened in 1985 as an outdoor amphitheater for live shows and concerts.

RIGHT: In the 1960s, Walt Disney conceived a magnificent ski resort and recreation area he hoped to build at Mineral King in the mountains of Northern California. Though this 1969 sketch and many others were created to show how the project would blend seamlessly into the natural environment, a series of legal tangles prevented the project from ever being built.

"I look at flies, at flowers, at leaves and trees around me. I let my mind drift at ease, just like a boat in the current. Sooner or later, it is caught by something."

—PABLO PICASSO

ABOVE: Giant glass domes dominate this vision for Disney Sea, conceived as a new theme park to be built along the ocean in Long Beach, California. Inside the domes, guests would experience the worlds of the sea. Outside, many ocean and water themed attractions, including a thrilling journey through the heart of an undersea volcano, would entertain visitors. This concept later served as inspiration for Tokyo Disney Sea.

LEFT: As part of a proposed International Food Pavilion for World Showcase at Epcot, Herbert Ryman created this sketch for the House of Cheese. Sharp as it was, the concept had to be sliced from the original Epcot menu. And it's a Gouda thing, too. It would have been a real Muenster to build.

BELOW: In 1951, the very first concept sketches created for Disneyland included a haunted house. The Imagineers combined countless versions of such an attraction into the Haunted Mansion, which opened in 1969. One idea didn't make it into the final attraction—The Museum of the Weird, shown here in this 1964 concept sketch by Rolly Crump. The Haunted Mansion was originally envisioned as a walking tour, which would have concluded inside the Museum.

Where will it go? What will it be? For now, it remains but our fantasy.

GOOD IDEAS NEVER GO AWAY

At Imagineering, a good idea is a precious commodity whether developed right away or not. Even when an idea does not make it to the initial design or building stage, it is never forgotten. It may turn up sometime later for use in some other project, in part, or in its entirety. Here are a few examples of what we mean when we say good ideas never go away.

"Get a good idea and stay with it. Dog it and work at it until it's done, and done right."

—WALT DISNEY

If the spark of an idea is strong, it will never fade away. Even if it travels only far enough to appear on that first piece of paper, there it will patiently remain until the time is right for it to re-ignite.

RIGHT AND BELOW: **In 1974, Tony Baxter created this vision of Discovery Bay (right), a-turn-of-the-century scientific outpost built in the style of San Francisco's Barbary Coast. Visitors would experience the worlds of such famous science fiction authors as Jules Verne and H. G. Wells, exploring the deep sea aboard Captain Nemo's submarine *Nautilus*, and looping upside-down on a magnetic roller-coaster. While Discovery Bay has yet to appear along the Rivers of America in Disneyland's Frontierland, the *Nautilus* and *Hyperion* have found a home in Discoveryland at Disneyland Paris, as seen in this rendering by Tim Delaney (below).**

RIGHT AND FAR RIGHT: **An early vision for the grand dream that became known as the Experimental Prototype Community of Tomorrow (EPCOT) is seen in this rendering (far right) by Herbert Ryman. The concept was born in Walt Disney's mind and first visualized as "Progress City" decades before he had the means to devise this plan. While Progress City was never built, a spectacular scale model was presented as the finale to Carousel of Progress at Disneyland. Today, the model can still be viewed from aboard the Tomorrowland Transit Authority in the Magic Kingdom at Walt Disney World.**

BELOW: **Echoing the past while dreaming of the future, Walt Disney proudly points to a detailed overview of his city of the future, just as he did with Peter Ellenshaw's rendering of Disneyland a decade earlier. As Walt envisioned it, people would actually live and work in Epcot—an idea that is coming true thirty years later at Celebration, a community of homes, shops and workplaces built on a portion of the Walt Disney World property.**

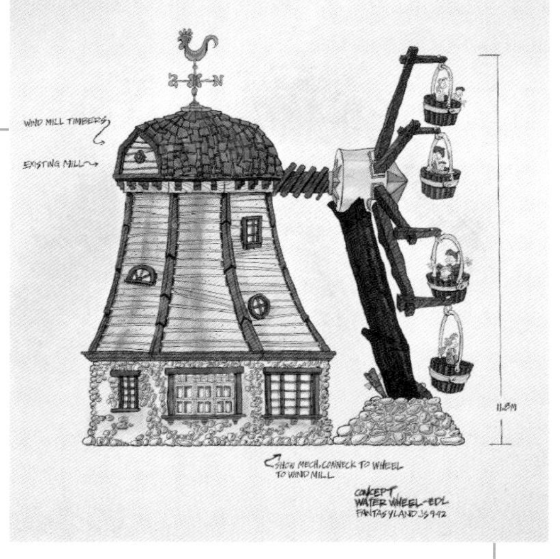

LEFT AND ABOVE: **Designer Bruce Bushman's 1954 concept for a windmill Ferris wheel (left), inspired by Walt Disney's Silly Symphony cartoon *The Old Mill*, was originally proposed for Fantasyland at Disneyland. Forty years later, as seen in this sketch by Jim Shull (above), the idea finally came to life in 1993 at Disneyland Paris—courtesy of Imagineer Tom Morris, who had remembered seeing the original sketch two decades earlier.**

CHAPTER 2 # THE FANTASY

Brainstorms provide our spark with a solid foundation upon which we build a definitive design. Though we can imagine the end result, the concept is a long way from reality. Our next step involves a little more imagination—and a lot more blank paper—as we define the details of the idea, and determine how it can best emerge to tell its story in a three-dimensional world.

Sketches are pinned onto large storyboards. Dozens of them are added, taken away, switched around, re-drawn, crumpled up and tossed out, then fetched from the trash can, uncrumpled, and put back up.

Clay is molded, foam is carved, and cardboard and plastic are cut and glued together to bring the idea into three dimensions. Creating small-scale study models both validates the strength of the concept and reveals its weaknesses. Preliminary models invite us to meet these design challenges head-on by providing a dimensional proving ground for changes and innovative solutions. (There is no such thing as a problem at Imagineering—only a challenge.)

Several generations of study models are built and rebuilt. First draft scripts undergo second and third revisions. Definitive sketches are generated by the dozens. Computers conjure up evolving visions of next-generation ride systems, architectural masses and scene-by-scene set possibilities.

As these individual efforts come together, so too, does our idea. Frequently, the developing concept looks nothing like its first sketch. Sometimes it looks exactly the same. Regardless of the outcome, the growing concept exists courtesy of its original spark.

There is more to our design process than pleasing the concept team. A major part of development is pitching the idea to management. Presentations are made at various intervals of concept development, to get further direction and continued approval. Concept presentations usually feature the latest artwork and storyboards which the team uses to explain the idea to leaders from Imagineering, the theme parks and The Walt Disney Company.

Sometimes our pitches are not quite on target and we strike

Floating between luminous clouds of endless possibilities and our unbounded imaginations, the idea grows wherever it goes. In the beginning, the only thing we do not allow in our world of fantasy is a tight pull on the tether of practicality.

LEFT: This 1976 rendering by Herbert Ryman is one of the very few pieces of original art created during the development of Tokyo Disneyland, since most of the park was similar in design to its California and Florida siblings. However, here we see a key difference: in contrast to the intimate scale of Disneyland, this view shows the park's vast open spaces, created to provide a sense of relief from the tightly congested streets of nearby Tokyo.

BELOW: Sometimes the Imagineers can take an idea and literally turn it around backwards to create something new, as seen here in Sam McKim's 1986 view of the reverse drop that sends guests sailing backwards down a waterfall in the Norway pavilion at World Showcase.

OPPOSITE BELOW: When Imagineers Tony Baxter and Chris Tietz first thought about gathering together the Swiss Family Treehouse, Captain Hook's Pirate Ship and the giant Skull Rock to form an Adventure Isle at Disneyland Paris, they asked artist Dan Goozee to create this rendering to convey the concept to others—and to convince themselves that the idea would actually work!

out (but we have a lot of drawing boards around here we can go back to). Sometimes we never even get to bat.

For those projects that result in home runs, small-scale study models quickly evolve into large-scale, finely detailed depictions of what the idea may one day become. Quick studies in clay give way to intricately sculpted maquettes, small-sized versions of what could become full-sized Audio-Animatronics characters. Computer-generated ride vehicle designs gear-up to roll off the electronic screen and into the shop. Confident ink lines trace over rough pencil lines on storyboard panels. Final draft scripts are ready for the recording studio, musical arrangements are written, and the movie cameras are ready to roll. Loose drawings, ready to be tightened into blueprints and conceptual sketches, can be rendered into fine art. The diamond in the rough is about to emerge as a multi-faceted gem.

All the elements necessary to tell the story of Br'er Rabbit's escape down the waterfall and into the briar patch below can be found in this 1990 concept rendering for Splash Mountain at Tokyo Disneyland, by artist John Horny.

While dreaming and scheming, we give the idea shape, whatever it might be for now. We ignore any obstacles it may present, for we are not yet concerned with how.

ABOVE: The storyboards are always kept close at hand as the design process continues. Here, Imagineers Scott Goddard and Daniel Singer (seated) use the boards as reference while transforming these two-dimensional drawings into the three-dimensional world of Splash Mountain.

RIGHT: Imagineers Steve Humke, Yoshi Akiyama and Ann Malmlund put the finishing touches on the overall exterior scale model of Splash Mountain for Tokyo Disneyland. From this point on, the model will be the "bible" of shape, style and color for the design and production of the attraction.

Telling the Story

The first step in developing a three-dimensional world is to see it in two-dimensional storyboards. It's a tradition that dates back to the earliest days of film animation and is used to this day at both the Feature Animation Studios and at Imagineering. Storyboards are large wood-framed panels upon which artists pin conceptual sketches while developing story sequences. The uniformly-sized boards are hung in logical sequence on the wall for continued story development, subsequent presentations, and eventually, as reference guides in the production of a film.

For each ride, show, or attraction, a logical story sequence is created. Almost every aspect of a project is broken down into progressive scene sketches, called storyboard panels, that reflect the beginning, middle, and end of our guests' park experience.

The boards are eventually covered with every written thought, idea, and rough sketch we can come up with. If need be, a separate set of storyboards is developed for the sole purpose of establishing the camera shots required for the videos or film that may be part of the attraction. As they are fine-tuned, the boards are used as a presentation tool to sell the idea to management, and to explain the concept to all of the Imagineering departments that will contribute to the evolution of the project.

A completed storyboard offers us the first chance to experience a new ride or show and see how the idea might—or might not—work.

"Only in men's imagination does every truth find an effective and undeniable existence. Imagination, not invention, is the supreme master of art as of life."

—JOSEPH CONRAD

LEFT: Animation drawings like these sketches of Br'er Bear and Br'er Fox by artist Joe Lanzisero provide details of figure positions and movements which will help the sculptors and animators bring the story to life.

BELOW: In addition to conveying the storyline of an attraction, storyboards (like this one created by Joe Lanzisero for Splash Mountain) define such diverse elements as the character poses, the mood, color styling, the scenery and the props.

"We have never lost faith in family entertainment—stories that make people laugh, stories about warm and human things, stories about historic characters and events, and stories about animals."

—WALT DISNEY

THE STORY BEHIND THE STORY

Everything we do at Imagineering is driven by story. When an idea for a show, attraction or entire theme park is in development, an Imagineering team creates a story behind the story or a back story which plays a big role in further defining the details of the project.

When a myth or legend is created, it may present itself in the form of a basic outline, oral or written story, or even a poem. Because it is primarily a design aid—an inside story told only within the halls of Imagineering—the mythology may never actually be made known to our park guests. But it is there to support the structure of the story just as steel, wood and concrete support its physical structure.

Often, the names of characters, places and things that first appear in the myth will show up in the attraction. Here are a few of our favorite back stories.

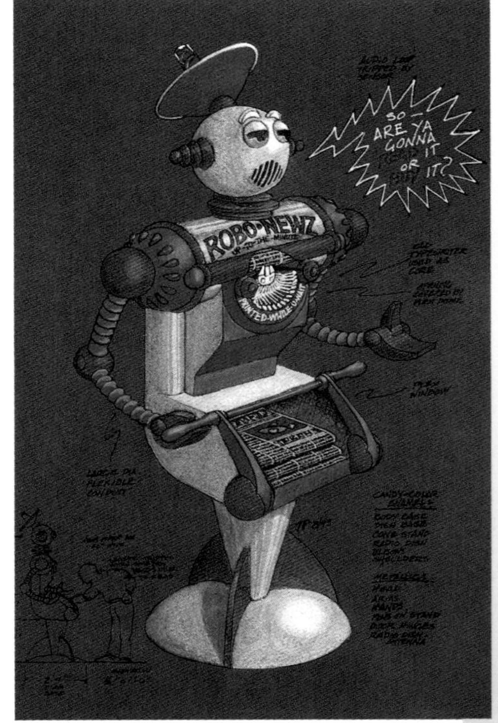

"Tomorrowland—Headquarters for the League of Planets" art by Thom Flowers, 1993

At the Walt Disney World Magic Kingdom, Tomorrowland is a community where everyday living is made better through science, invention and intergalactic influence. Inhabited by robots, space aliens and a few humans, this amazing Earth community is so world-renowned, it was selected as the universal headquarters for the League of Planets.

In Tomorrowland, robots perform household chores, ice cream comes from the Milky Way, and a trip through time is as common as a spin around the solar system. Tomorrowlanders keep up with the latest on and off-world wonders and technologies by visiting the exhibits presented at their neighborhood Interplanetary Convention and Science Centers.

Those who work and play in and around Rockettower Plaza, the bustling heart of the community, live outside of town in the hoverburbs. They commute via the Tomorrowland Transit Authority's Superskyway Blueline Express. Locals get all the news before it even happens by subscribing to the Tomorrowland Times.

Today, in this fantasy community of Tomorrow, the future that never was is alive and well.

"It Was Our Pleasure" art by Chris Carradine

Pleasure Island at Walt Disney World Village was an abandoned industrial waterfront district that was converted into a nightclub complex. The property was originally owned by one Merriweather Pleasure, a seafaring adventurer, who, during the nineteenth century, operated Pleasure's Canvas and Sailmaking, Inc. His business became the heart of Pleasure Island, a place to which daring adventurers from all over the globe came to tell their incredible tales.

But Merriweather was not a landlubber at heart, and hearing these stories made him long once again for adventure on the high seas. One day, he heeded the haunting call of the bounding main, and set sail from Pleasure Island. Upon learning that their father was lost at sea, Pleasure's two lazy sons abandoned the business. The once bustling waterfront district was left to decay beside a mysterious lagoon. Years later, the near-ruins of Pleasure Island were rediscovered by adventurous Imagineers with their own incredible tales to tell.

These Imagineers refurbished the island, turning its run-down warehouses into exciting restaurants and nightclubs that were designed to reflect the original themes of Pleasure's functional buildings. Once again, the district bustles with the activity of world travelers who come together in the spirit of fun and adventure; a tradition established here a century ago.

"The Miner Details of Big Thunder"

art by J. Demeis, 1975

Big Thunder Mountain Railroad dates back to the wild and woolly boom town days when every prospector west of the Rockies was looking for gold. The following is the tall tale heard tell by one of those prospectors who got it second-hand from old Sam, the last of the Big Thunder Miners:

Yessir, it is 1840, and around these parts, things got prit' near quiet as the hangin' tree on Sunday after the Big Thunder Mine tapped out. One day there ain't none richer, the next, even a ghost wouldn't have much innerst in her.

Things got mighty busted up and rusted down inside Big Thunder, so Sam told me while sluggin' from a dusty bottle of Old Imagineer. He was the last prospector inside that mine. Fact is, poor old Sam took a spill and done landed belly up in one of them ore cars. Next thing he knows, the car takes off like a skinny coyote after a plump hen!

Off he went, a headin' fer the mine. Seems like that old ghost mine came to life for Sam. He swears the rusted winch engine was a pumpin' and a wheezin' and just when he was thinkin' he must have bats in his belfry, there was bats! Then he sat up to see what he could see in the dark, and there was pools of rainbow water and waterfalls, and plenty of them rocks the schoolmarm calls "stalactites and stalagmites."

The walls of the canyon kept comin' in closer and closer at old Sam and he yelled until he couldn't yell no more. All of a sudden, the car thunders into a pitch dark tunnel, with Sam holdin' on fer dear life. Comin' back out the other side, he spots a couple a danged skunks foolin' with blastin' powder, like to blow the top off a whole derned mountain! Little ways away, danged if'n there ain't a Billy goat chawin' on a stick of the stuff! But Sam didn't have no time to worry about that, 'cuz next thing he knows he's whippin' down Spiral Butte and headin' right back down into Big Thunder Mine. Sam figgered he was goin' in and never comin' out this time, with all that rumblin' and shakin' and rocks comin' down all around him. He closed his eyes tight but the next thing ya know he was outside and high-ballin' down on the track again, right over the Bear River Trestle Bridge.

That ore car finally squealed to a stop right smack dab in the middle of Big Thunder Town. Sam just sat up, brushed off the dust and said, "I ain't had this much of a whoop and a holler since the Grub Gang hit town. I just barely got out with my hide!"

Sam's amazing ghost story was told and retold over the years, and because of it, no one was ever brave enough to even set foot near the mine—until the day a bold young Imagineer heard the tale and thought it might be fun to take a ride on old Big Thunder himself. Sure enough, he did, and the train ride turned out to be so much fun he decided to officially re-open the mine. Folks soon heard the news about Big Thunder and began to arrive there to take their own wild ride on the legendary runaway train.

"Mickey's Swell Idea" art by Don Carson, 1990

Of course, everyone knows that Mickey's Toontown existed long before Disneyland was built right next door. One happy day in 1952, while Walt Disney was in Toontown visiting his pal Mickey Mouse, his dream for a new park came up in conversation. Mickey knew that whenever Walt got that sparkle in his eye, whatever he was dreaming up was bound to come true. So he was dismayed when Walt confided in him that he was having a difficult time finding a site large enough to accommodate all the wonderful things he had in mind.

"Oh, boy, I've got a swell idea!" Mickey exclaimed as he grabbed Walt by the hand and led him over to the fence that separated Toontown from the human world. "Take a look over this fence," continued Mickey. "There's a fine and dandy parcel of land just on the other side that would be a wonderful place to build Disneyland!" And it was.

Many years went by before it finally dawned on the toons (the first time something dawned on them besides a happy cartoon sun) that since it was so easy for them to go next door to visit all their non-toon friends at Disneyland, their non-toon friends could just as easily come visit them in Toontown! And that is exactly what happened when Mickey's Toontown was "finally" opened to Disneyland visitors in February, 1993.

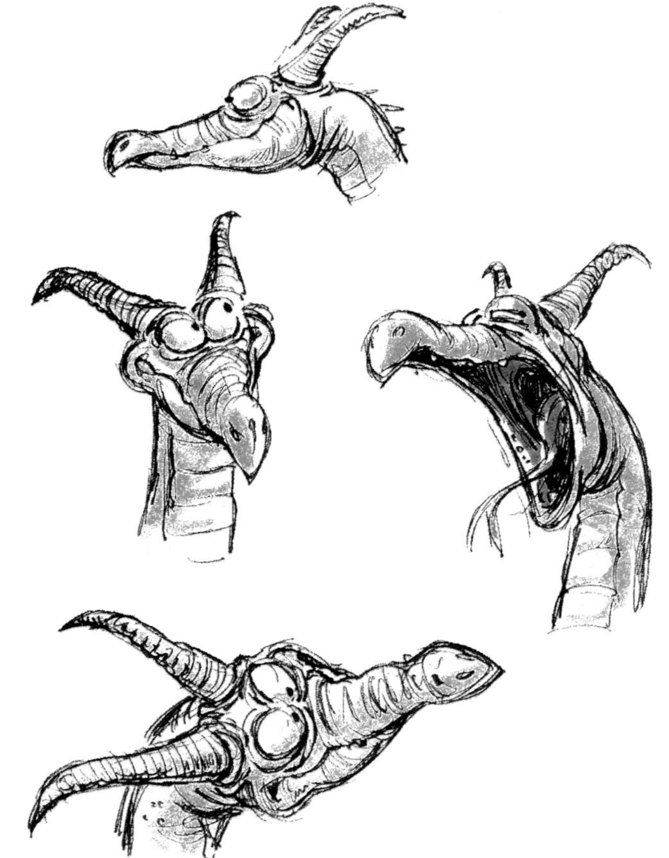

"Each sculpture has its own requirements, depending on size, shape and whether or not it will be kinetic. If the figure will be animated, we need to be concerned about how the mechanics will fit inside the figure. We also have to keep in mind where the joints will pivot, and have a broad understanding of anatomy and range of motion."

—VALERIE EDWARDS

ABOVE: Sometimes the look of a character inspires its name—and sometimes the name inspires the character. In this case, a figment of the imagination became Figment the mischievous dragon, as visualized by artist Andy Gaskill in 1979.

BELOW: Newly created characters Dreamfinder and Figment have a good chuckle over the shoulders of Barry Braverman, Tony Baxter and Julie Svendsen, who are busy puzzling out how best to use these new characters to tell the story of Imagination.

CHARACTER BUILDING

Once a ride or show concept has been determined, the next step we take is to "populate" the newly created world. Just as Feature Animation develops characters to tell their stories in film, we develop characters to tell our stories in theme parks. A 90-minute film, however, allows plenty of time to develop the personality, motivation and enduring qualities, whether good or bad, of a character. Because of the relatively short length of a theme park attraction, all of the ingredients that make up a character and his or her role in the show must be recognized almost immediately.

In rides like Snow White's Adventures, Peter Pan's Flight or Dumbo the Flying Elephant, the characters are the same as those already established in film and are therefore instantly recognized and accepted in a three-dimensional role. At the same time, they bring to the ride a "built-in" mythology and design theme based upon the story developed at length in their respective films. The same holds true for historical personalities portrayed in our parks, such as Ben Franklin and Will Rogers, for example, who appear in the American Adventure at Epcot. But when characters are exclusive to a theme park ride or show, they must be able to effectively represent a theme and tell the stories of their attractions in no time at all.

Whether they appear on a theatrical stage, as part of an attraction, or in our many films or videos, the "stars" of our shows range from realistic animals to fantasy creatures, sleek futuristic robots to human beings—with a few fruits and vegetables tossed in! After they are designed on paper, our characters come to life in many forms, including Audio-Animatronics figures, puppets, traditional cel or computer-generated animation, live actors playing roles on film or even as "walk-around" costumed characters.

Many of our Audio-Animatronics "actors" assume major theatrical roles by taking on the enormous responsibility of acting-out a script. Others merely add to an overall story in combination with the action occurring within a sequence of ride sets. In a few cases, an entire show may be based upon the performance of a single character without an elaborate background or any other action at all, as is the case with "stand-up comedians" Alec Tronic at Innoventions at Epcot and Otto Matic at The Disney Store on Fifth Avenue in New York City, and intergalactic "lounge singer" Sonny Eclipse, who entertains patrons of Cosmic Ray's Starlight Cafe in the Magic Kingdom at Walt Disney World.

Some of our characters are created exclusively for theme park videos or big-screen films, such as Chairman Clench, the space alien corporate executive played by Jeffrey Jones for the ExtraTERRORestrial Alien Encounter at the Magic Kingdom in Walt Disney World, Captain EO, played by Michael Jackson, or Dr. Nigel Channing of the Imagination Institute played by Eric Idle for the Honey I Shrunk the Audience attraction in Epcot. On rare occasions, a character may appear both on film and as an Audio-Animatronics figure, as does Buzzy, star of the Cranium Command show in Wonders of Life at Epcot.

Many of our theme park performers have become classic Disney characters, including Big Al of Country Bear Jamboree, Figment and Dreamfinder of the Imagination pavilion at Epcot, the children from It's A Small World, the rascal crew from Pirates of the Caribbean, the four Enchanted Tiki Birds, Jose, Michael, Pierre and Fritz, Trader Sam of Jungle Cruise fame, Rex, the wacky robot pilot on Star Tours, Timekeeper from Le Visionarium at Disneyland Paris and the Timekeeper show at the Walt Disney World Magic Kingdom, and even Ice Gator, the blue alligator mascot of Blizzard Beach.

Whatever form they may take, in whatever show or attraction they may appear, each of our stars has greatly contributed to giving our parks a most memorable character.

ABOVE: **Hitchhiking ghosts try to scare up a ride home, in this 1968 Haunted Mansion concept sketch by Marc Davis.**

ABOVE RIGHT: **Captain Cortex prepares to pilot a human mind through the course of a day's events in artist X. Atencio's 1987 concept sketch for Cranium Command. By the time the show opened in 1989 in Wonders of Life at Epcot, the Captain Cortex character had been refined, and in the process was renamed Buzzy.**

RIGHT: **The key to the Pirates' problem is almost within reach, in this 1964 concept sketch for Pirates of the Caribbean by Marc Davis.**

BELOW RIGHT: **Imagineer Jeff Burke refines the characters for Kitchen Kabaret, an Epcot attraction that took a look at the many food groups making up a nutritious meal. A decade later, tastes had changed—so a fresh menu of characters was cooked up to star in a new revue, Food Rocks, as seen in this poster design (below) by Rennie Marquez.**

"My favorite sculpting tools are my hands. Of all the tools, the hands are the most sensitive. The head, though, is always the main sculpting tool. It is where all the imagination and inspiration begins."

—BLAINE GIBSON

LEFT AND BELOW: **Early concept sketches by Joe Rohde for Fuzzball and Hooter, as they get ready to help Captain Eo spread music and beauty throughout the universe.**

"The things we sculpted may have been animated mechanically, but if they already had a spark of life inherent in their conceptualization, then they worked even better."

—BLAINE GIBSON

BELOW: **In 1973, Marc Davis created Sam the Eagle and his unnamed owl friend as the hosts for America Sings, a Disneyland journey through the history of American music. When the attraction closed in 1988, it seemed that typecasting must be inevitable in any actor's life—the pair had become so recognizable they were the only two left behind when the rest of the America Sings Audio-Animatronics figures were "recast" as characters in Splash Mountain.**

LEFT AND BELOW: When the concept of a Star Tours "intergalactic tour bus" was proposed in a brainstorming session with filmmaker George Lucas, Imagineer Chris Runco came up with a robot called RX-24—Rex for short—your inexperienced guide and pilot. (Below) Chris works on a full-size dimensional model of Rex , whose final appearance is shown in this sketch by Gil Keppler (left).

"Our sculpture studio is full of life. It is a little museum containing the histories of all the Disney Theme Parks."

—ADOLFO PROCOPIO

Imagineering is home to all forms of artistic expression. Like individual parts that are joined together to form one whole, each of us joins together to contribute to the whole of the idea.

LEFT: This concept rendering for Sonny Eclipse was created by Dave Feiten to illustrate how the intergalactic "lounge lizard" might appear while entertaining restaurant patrons in Cosmic Ray's Starlight Cafe Lounge in Tomorrowland at the Magic Kingdom. The story behind Sonny is that he was discovered by restaurateur Cosmic Ray while performing his "Bossa Supernova" musical stylings at cosmic weddings and space mall openings all over the galaxy.

RIGHT AND BOTTOM: **The Marc Davis concept sketches that made Walt laugh.**

BELOW: **Marc Davis, Claude Coats and X. Atencio carry on development of the Country Bears "after Walt." Together, they would complete the bear show Walt loved so much, as well as create the concepts for such legendary Imagineering attractions as Pirates of the Caribbean and the Haunted Mansion.**

"Walt would always spontaneously drop into your room to chat and see how you were doing. By the time he left, you were fired up with excitement about whatever it was you were working on."

—FRED JOERGER

WALT'S LAST LAUGH

In 1966, as Imagineer Marc Davis was creating character designs and storyboard sketches for a new attraction, he was paid a special and memorable visit. At the time, plans were in the works for a park development in Northern California called Mineral King. Marc, an animator turned Imagineer, was developing ideas for an Audio-Animatronics musical revue for Mineral King that would feature a cast of country music-singing bears. Whenever Marc was deeply involved with an idea, he would literally cover his office walls with sketches.

One day, as Walt so often did, he stopped in to see what Marc was up to. From literally hundreds of pinned-up sketches, he immediately singled one out that featured a bear playing a tuba, and began to laugh hysterically. He told Marc, between guffaws, that he "really had a winner here with these musical bears."

As Walt began to leave the office, he turned and said, "Good-bye, Marc." This took the artist by surprise as Walt never said good-bye, but rather, always said, "so long" or "see ya." Walt died a few days later. Marc believes this was the last time Walt ever had a good laugh.

The Mineral King project was eventually canceled, but the musical bears refused to go into concept hibernation. In 1971, they made their debut at Walt Disney World, where they put on a hand-clappin', foot stompin' centerpiece show called Country Bear Jamboree.

Since they made their first stage appearance, those "musical bears" have entertained millions of guests at Walt Disney World, Disneyland, and Tokyo Disneyland. The echo of Walt's laugh can still be heard today.

ABOVE: Dorothea Redmond created the styling for the interior of the Country Bear Playhouse, seen above in the 1970 rendering that provided inspiration for the creation of the actual theater (above right).

RIGHT: Marc Davis originally created the character of Trixie the Bear as a circus performer (near right). As the design progressed, she became the more demure and refined songstress we know today (far right).

BACKGROUND: Walt Disney.

RIGHT: This interior color sketch of the Netherlands, by Mary Blair, set the style for the countries of the world portrayed in It's a Small World.

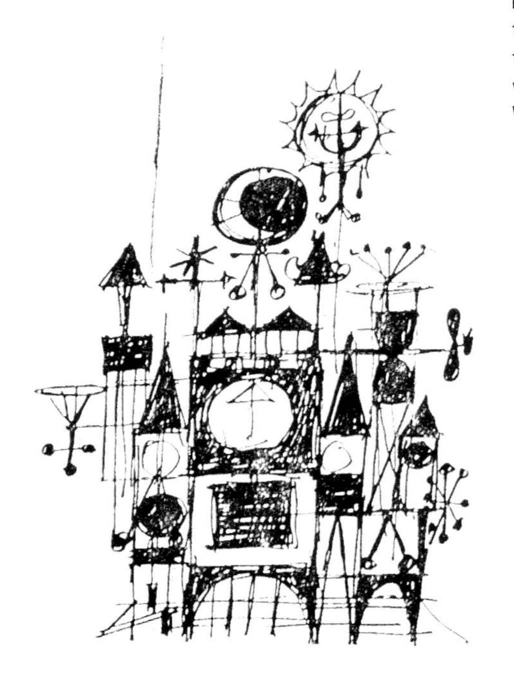

ABOVE: Walt asked artist, illustrator and color stylist Mary Blair to design a clock tower for the entrance to It's a Small World at Disneyland. On a plane flying to Los Angeles from her home in New York, Mary created this sketch on a small scrap of paper—a sketch that became the inspiration for the Small World facade.

BELOW: This is one of a pair of sketches that provided the original color styling for the exterior of It's a Small World at Disneyland. Mary was famous for her contemporary, leading edge—yet charming—designs. In the 30 years since these designs were created, the Imagineers have attempted to follow her example, updating the color schemes to be equally appealing to the audiences of today.

A CERTAIN STYLE

When Walt Disney agreed to create It's A Small World for the 1964 New York World's Fair, he recalled the series of drawings of Mexican children that had been used for the "La Piñata" sequence of his animated film *The Three Caballeros*. He thought the unique style of the art would lend itself perfectly to the design of the entire ride.

The artist, Mary Blair, had been a color stylist and designer at the Disney Studios during the 1940s, and had gone on to become an illustrator of children's books. Walt invited her to come back, challenging her to design the new attraction in the same charming style she created for the "La Piñata" sequence.

Upon Mary's return, she was joined by designers Marc Davis, Alice Davis, and Rolly Crump to translate her unique "La Piñata" style into three dimensions. With less than nine months before the fair's opening day, time was of the essence. Fortunately, Mary's original drawings for *The Three Caballeros* immediately established the style and mood intended for the attraction, providing the designers with the solid creative focus they needed to move the project ahead. In the meantime, Robert B. and Richard M. Sherman were inspired by the drawings as they wrote the now famous theme song.

Layer upon layer, we create a patchwork of sketches and words that color the original idea. Funny, fantastic, diverting, enhancing, persuasive, serious or not, our visualized thoughts begin to chisel away and uncover the diamond in the rough.

"The key to the success of It's A Small World was that in creating it, we all remained faithful to the mood and feel of Mary's design."

—ROLLY CRUMP

ABOVE: Calling on his background as an animator for the Disney Studios, Marc Davis created this model sheet to illustrate the movements he envisioned for the Children of the World in It's a Small World.

TOP: It's a Small World debuted at Disneyland in 1966, adorned with a beautiful animated facade inspired by this concept sketch from artist Mary Blair.

ABOVE RIGHT: Mary Blair created this character sketch for the 1945 Walt Disney film *The Three Caballeros*. Almost 20 years later, Walt still remembered this sketch, and used it as the inspiration for the singing children in It's a Small World.

RIGHT: This very early sketch by Marc Davis is an example of how he developed a unique personality for each of the children in It's a Small World.

ABOVE: Walt Disney challenged his designers to represent cultures from all over the world in a single attraction, It's a Small World. In this 1963 rendering, Marc Davis attempted to demonstrate how the diverse environments of Africa could be captured in a single scene.

LEFT: Mary Blair, seen here developing the color styling for It's a Small World in 1963. Mary's unique sense of color graced many children's books in the 1950s and 1960s. Her designs were a favorite of Walt Disney, who called her in to contribute to such classic animated features as Cinderella and Alice in Wonderland. Mary would also contribute designs for the colorful ceramic tile murals in Tomorrowland at Disneyland and in the Contemporary Resort Hotel at the Walt Disney World Resort.

BELOW LEFT: Mary Blair, creating more of her unique color stylings.

ABOVE: Poster created in 1970 by Mary Blair from a concept by Paul Hartley to promote the opening of It's a Small World in the Magic Kingdom at the Walt Disney World Resort.

OPPOSITE: These were the very first character sketches created for It's a Small World by Marc Davis, to suggest which countries might be featured and how their children might be portrayed.

RUSSIA
BALKANS
BELGIUM
JAPAN
INDIA
NORTH POLE
MIDDLE EAST

ABOVE: Walt Disney's life-long fascination with all forms of transportation inspired "A World on the Move" as the theme for the 1967 opening of New Tomorrowland at Disneyland. In this concept rendering by Herbert Ryman, we see the WEDWay PeopleMover ("the transportation system that never stops") making its way past the towering SpacePort.

WINDOWS INTO THE FUTURE

Walt Disney Imagineering is not an art museum, but we do have one of the largest and finest collections of original paintings in the world. The artists who have dedicated their lives and talents to Disney dreams may not be world-famous, but their work is our greatest treasure.

A concept painting is an open window to the future, offering an exciting glimpse of the concept as it might someday appear. These works are completed during the earliest stages of a project's development, loosely based on a smattering of fresh and unrefined information. Yet, they are often used later as a source for color and material selection, and as inspiration for model building, set, landscape and lighting design, and even architectural plans and elevations.

It is no wonder then, that even though a concept painting is finished years before the actual project becomes real, its glimpse into the future can be remarkably accurate.

RIGHT: The mysterious jungle moods of the Explorer's Club restaurant in Adventureland at Disneyland Paris are effectively conveyed in this 1988 rendering by Bryan Jowers.

"The real artist's work is a surprise to himself. The big painter is the one who has something to say. He thus does not paint men, landscape or furniture, but an idea."

–ROBERT HENRI
American Painter

ABOVE: The Snow Queen comes to life in this concept sketch by Marc Davis, inspiration for The Ice Palace, a winter wonderland proposed for the Walt Disney World Resort. This sketch was one of the last drawn by Marc Davis before his retirement from Imagineering in 1978.

LEFT: This very first rendering for Tokyo Disney Seas, painted in 1993 by Scott Sinclair, attempts to establish the time period, theme and emotional feeling of the new park. Renderings like this one would be used to inspire other designers and provide them with a sense of direction.

There is nothing we do here that is not creative. There is nothing creative that we do not do here.

BELOW: The success of Epcot at the Walt Disney World Resort inspired many concepts for a west-coast version of the park. One of those concepts—called Westcot—is seen here in this 1993 rendering by R. Tom Gilleon. The spire at left would mark the entrance to a celebration of the technologies and lifestyles of tomorrow, surrounded by intimate recreations of the countries and cultures of the world.

ABOVE: This very early concept rendering of the Africa Safari, created by Ben Tripp, shows how very different Disney's Animal Kingdom would be—wide open spaces, total authenticity and real, live animals.

TOP: This concept for a boat ride in Disney's Animal Kingdom owes its inspiration to the Jungle Cruise at Disneyland—but this time its inhabitants would be very much alive, as shown in this concept sketch by Joe Rohde.

ABOVE: In this 1953 sketch, Herbert Ryman created the first visualization of Sleeping Beauty Castle, which would grace the entrance to Fantasyland at Disneyland. The design was inspired by Neuschwanstein Castle in Bavaria, but Walt Disney felt this interpretation was a little too realistic. At a design review of a model based on this sketch, the top half of the castle was turned around backwards—and a world renowned landmark was born. At top left, Walt Disney points to this same sketch as he introduces Disneyland to the world in 1954.

BELOW: At Disneyland Paris, Main Street stands as a recreation of turn-of-the-century America. To provide a historical reference for the European audience, fanciful murals adorn the interiors along the street. This mural by Dan Goozee recounts the fictional history of the Plaza Inn restaurant.

ABOVE LEFT: In this 1955 sketch, artist Sam McKim illustrates a turn-of-the-century drugstore on Main Street at Disneyland. This drawing, created during the early development of Disneyland, marks a rare instance when a concept sketch was based on an already-completed set of architectural blueprints—a sequence that would later be reversed to allow the architects to take their inspiration from already completed concept sketches. This reversal of the traditional design process plays a key role in the uniqueness of many Imagineering projects.

ABOVE RIGHT: Artist Sam McKim at work in 1993. After a lengthy career as childhood motion picture actor "Sammy McKim" (where he starred in countless western serials with Gene Autry) Sam came to Imagineering, designing much of the original Main Street and Frontierland at Disneyland. Sam is perhaps best known as the creator of the Disneyland Souvenir Maps, issued between 1958 and 1964. Sam's intricate and fascinating maps are among the most sought-after pieces of Disney memorabilia. In 1992, Sam created a new map in his unique style to commemorate the opening of Disneyland Paris.

OVERLEAF: Herbert Ryman created this 1980 rendering for The Heartbeat of Africa, the theme show for a proposed African pavilion in World Showcase.

ABOVE: This painting by Nina Rae Vaughn conveys the wild excitement a 3-D Muppet film adventure would bring to the Disney-MGM Studios—at a very early point when the actual concept for the film had not yet been developed.

ABOVE RIGHT: Artist Dorothea Redmond created five scenic arches for Cinderella Castle in the Magic Kingdom at the Walt Disney World Resort. In this arch, she included caricatures of John Hench (below right) and Herbert Ryman (below far right), two of the original—and most influential—Disney Imagineers.

ABOVE: This rendering for Typhoon Lagoon, created in 1989 by artist R. Tom Gilleon, shows how it's possible to convey a complete story in one single image. Renderings such as this one are a key element in conveying the ideas behind a new concept—and are invaluable in building excitement about the possibilities such a project might hold.

BELOW: Among the interior treatments found inside the 50,000 square foot "The World of Disney" shop located at the Walt Disney World Village are murals featuring Disney characters in humorous global situations. The gag in this concept rendering, a collaborative effort by Stuart Bailey and Maggie Parr, is as plain as the nose on Goofy's face.

ABOVE: The theater district from the Golden Age of Hollywood is brought back to life in this rendering of Sunset Boulevard at the Disney-MGM Studios by artist Bryan Jowers.

ABOVE RIGHT: This pirate's treasure map was created in 1988 by artist John Horny as part of the interior decor for the Blue Lagoon restaurant at Disneyland Paris. The map tells the story of Pirates of the Caribbean, and in caricature form pays tribute to the creators of the original Disneyland attraction.

RIGHT: The unique challenge of creating subtle artistic effects with glow-in-the-dark blacklight paint is able to be met by very few artists. Here, Imagineer Suzanne Rattigan lends her special skills to Snow White's Adventures for the Magic Kingdom at the Walt Disney World Resort.

LEFT: This poster by Albert Yu was created in 1996 for the first public announcement of Disney's California Adventure, a new theme park to be built adjacent to Disneyland.

BELOW: Walt Disney Imagineering Chairman Peter Rummell (center) reviews one of the concepts for Disney's California Adventure with President Ken Wong (left) and Vice Chairman Marty Sklar (right).

ABOVE: **Herbert Ryman created this aerial rendering of Frontierland at Disneyland in 1953, just as construction on the park was beginning.**

MAKING REAL HISTORY

The worlds we create on storyboards, in sculpted characters, and intricately detailed dimensional models can range from the wildest of fantasies to factual, historical and other realistic environments. Often recreating a realistic world can be a far greater challenge than dreaming up the wildest fantasy.

Walt Disney dearly loved America and her colorful history. He long held the belief that we, as Americans, should recognize the extraordinary influence of historical events on our present-day lives. In his strong desire to help Americans become more aware of the significance of their nation and its heritage, he included many aspects of its history and culture within Disneyland. But Walt was also aware of America's relationship with the rest of the world, and the importance of understanding the cultures of all peoples. In honor and in tribute of Walt, his dreams of America and the world, we continue to represent culture and history in our theme parks today and in our plans for the future.

LEFT: **The interior of the Golden Horseshoe Saloon (home of Slue Foot Sue and the Golden Horseshoe Revue) as drawn by Sam McKim in 1954.**

RIGHT: **In 1992, John Horny created this overall view of Frontierland as the stage curtain for the Lucky Nugget Saloon at Disneyland Paris.**

ABOVE: **Walt Disney poses next to the Disneyland Stage Coach, an icon of the Old West that was one of Walt's many passions. The stage coach lines carried guests through Frontierland at Disneyland from 1955 to 1959.**

RIGHT: **A friendly Indian Village awaits explorers along the Rivers of America at Disneyland, in this 1984 rendering by Sam McKim.**

ABOVE: When the early concepts for Disneyland were starting to take shape, Dale Hennesey created this 1953 sketch to illustrate how a turn-of-the-century town square might appear to guests entering the park. By the time the designs for Disneyland were complete a year later, the Opera House and City Hall (seen here at opposite edges of the scene) had traded places.

RIGHT: When Herbert Ryman composed this watercolor concept rendering for the New Orleans Square project at Disneyland in 1964, he included many elements that were authentic to the Louisiana city of the 19th Century. Among them were the two Sisters of Charity, a common sight in New Orleans during that era. Beginning with these nuns, pairs of figures became a recurring theme in Herbert's later paintings, including a pair of aliens in a Horizons rendering for Epcot. Imagineer Frank Armitage paid tribute to this rendering in 1989, when he brought the nuns back to visit his concept painting of the castle for Disneyland Paris (see page 80).

ABOVE: A classic view of an American waterfront, created by R. Tom Gilleon as an inspirational sketch for Tokyo Disney Sea.

OVERLEAF: The Blue Bayou Restaurant at Disneyland, painted in 1964 by Dorothea Redmond. In addition to being a fine place to dine, The Blue Bayou also provides a peaceful transition from the hectic "real world" of a busy day at Disneyland into the fantasy world of Pirates of the Caribbean.

SHOWCASING AMERICA

From the first civilized colonies of the East to the dusty boom towns of the West, from the quaint little villages of the North to the sleepy bayous of the South, many American architectural styles have been perfectly recreated—in stylized or realistic renditions—to house shops, restaurants or shows that carry the same themes inside.

BELOW: Herbert Ryman created these two 1969 renderings to establish the look of Liberty Square in the Magic Kingdom at the Walt Disney World Resort.

Creativity is the outlet of imagination. What we imagine is expressed by what we create. In our fantasy, what we create are pieces of dreams that awaken, one by one, to become the building blocks of the idea.

ABOVE: New citizens are processed through Ellis Island as a turn-of-the-century America celebrates the Fourth of July, in this inspirational sketch for Disney's America by Dan Goozee.

RIGHT: The famous battle between the *Merrimack* and the *Monitor* is captured in this rendering for Disney's America by R. Tom Gilleon. The idea for a "celebration of America" park is especially appealing to Michael Eisner. Although this idea has not gone beyond the concept stage, many Imagineers feel "its time will come."

ABOVE: **Imagineer Collin Campbell at work on concept renderings for Epcot. Collin began working at the Disney Studios when he was just 15 years old, and during the next fifty years contributed to a diverse array of projects ranging from the classic Disney animated features** *Lady and the Tramp* **and** *Sleeping Beauty* **to It's a Small World and Tokyo Disneyland.**

TOP: **In this early concept for World Showcase, painted by Collin Campbell in 1975, each participating country would occupy a segment of a giant pie-shaped building.**

Showcasing the World

World Showcase in Epcot at Walt Disney World was originally going to be a separate theme park. The idea was to combine representations of the nations of the world together within two huge twin structures that formed semi-circular malls. Each of the pavilions, visible only from the front, would be situated closely side-by-side, with their entrances open to the central core of the mall. In the first bird's-eye concept rendering, the pie-shaped pavilions attached to the main mall structures appeared much like airliners docked at an airport terminal.

The layout was considered so that each of the pavilions represented would appear to be the same size. Once through the front door, the pavilions could be extended in length as far as the country represented wished to sponsor. If a country wished to sponsor a ride, for example, it would be added to the building and could extend out back beyond the guests' sight.

Although sound in theory, the layout did not allow the designers to visually capture the ethnic essence of each of the participating countries. So the focus turned to the rich architectural diversity of each country. Each pavilion could be designed to present a look and style that reflected its ethnic architectural heritage. Not only would the pavilions be more visually excit-

ABOVE: **This 1975 rendering by Carlos Diniz shows World Showcase as a separate park, located adjacent to the Seven Seas Lagoon at Walt Disney World. Note its proximity to the Magic Kingdom.**

RIGHT: **This series of inspirational sketches by Dorothea Redmond (top two) and Harper Goff (bottom two) began to define the concept of an environmental World Showcase, with individually recognizable countries.**

ing from afar, they would be immediately recognizable as the country each represented.

The new design also eliminated an indoor-only guest experience by separating the once-attached, enclosed pavilions. Guests could meander outside each pavilion and experience the ambiance, music and architecture.

It was also decided that the World Showcase pavilions would belong to Epcot, forming a colorful league of nations around the scenic shores of a central lagoon.

Today, the neighboring pavilions provide a fun and unique way for guests to visit eleven countries in one day.

THESE PAGES: World Showcase pavilion concept paintings.

ABOVE: Canada by Bill Sulley.

TOP: China by Herbert Ryman.

LEFT: Germany by Bob Scifo.

BELOW LEFT: France by R. Tom Gilleon.

BELOW RIGHT: Japan by Bob Scifo.

ABOVE: Mexico by Collin Campbell.

ABOVE LEFT: American Adventure by Herbert Ryman.

LEFT: Norway by Collin Campbell.

BELOW: U.K. by Group West.

ABOVE: Morocco by Bob Scifo.

RIGHT: Italy by Herbert Ryman.

"Our main model shop should be designated a historical landmark. It has always been the design center of the company. Everything we built started right here in this room."

—ROLLY CRUMP

DESIGNING IN THREE DIMENSIONS

The modelmaker is the first Imagineer to make a concept real. The art of bringing a two-dimensional design into three dimensions is one of the most important and valued steps in the Imagineering process. Models enable us to visualize, in miniature, the physical layout and dimensions of a concept, and the relationships of show sets or buildings as they will appear. Viewing a project this way reveals a great deal about what works and what does not work. Models prompt questions. We are able to catch incongruities and make changes..

Every Imagineer involved in the evolution of a project uses its model as a guide. Models shed light on that which is hidden behind a flat concept rendering. They present the hard truth about what a project is, and what must be done to make it real. Walt Disney loved but did not rely on two-dimensional illustrations, as he believed they did not present the whole story.

In the development of a concept, the first models are simple ones fabricated from paper and foam blocks. Called massing models, their purpose is to introduce the idea to the dimensional world. These preliminary models demonstrate the relationships of every aspect of the project to each other, and allow for discussion, analysis and redesign as necessary.

As the project evolves, so too, do the models that represent it. Once the project team is satisfied with the arrangements portrayed on massing models, small-scale detail-oriented study models are begun. These reflect the architectural styles and colors for the project.

Creating a larger overall model, based upon detailed architectural and engineering drawings, is the last step in the model-making process. This show model is the exact replica of the project as it will be built, featuring the tiniest of details, including building exteriors, landscape, color schemes, the complete ride layout, vehicles, show sets, props, figures and suggested lighting and graphics.

Our models are carefully hand-crafted. Sophisticated technologies incorporate a new dimension to their dimensional design. With rigid precision, the

Anything can happen while we fantasize about the idea. It may even evolve into something entirely different from that which we first imagined. Whatever it becomes, the essence of that first spark will be forever responsible for its being.

"It's much easier for people to visualize a concept in three dimensions. You can't get inside a two-dimensional building. That's why we also use models in presentations, to sell the idea of the attraction."

—BILL VANEK

ABOVE: A massive project on the scale of Epcot is an incredibly complex undertaking. Everything above and below the ground must be agreed upon and coordinated. The design progresses from small-scale "massing models" (opposite left) to more detailed 1/500th scale models (center) and finally to a giant 1/8" scale model (right), which allows every design discipline to fully understand how each element of the project interacts.

TOP: As the large-scale model for Epcot was being built—and frequently revised—artists Clem Hall and Bob Scifo painted—and frequently revised—this spectacular aerial rendering of the park, a rare instance where a project's scale model was used as the primary reference for a concept rendering.

ABOVE: Walt Disney poses with the scale model of Matterhorn Mountain for Disneyland. After construction of the Matterhorn was completed in 1959, the model was discarded—and this is the only photograph of it known to exist.

shop's Laser Cam system cuts wood, plastic and paper pieces that are assembled to achieve the most intricate of details.

A camera the size of a lipstick tube is placed inside a model to relay a life-sized point-of-view. The imagery provided by the camera can be viewed in real time as it travels around inside the model, or recorded on videotape. Still photos also can be produced.

In addition to the three-dimensional models, we create the illusion of three dimensions with computers. Computer modeling allows us to see what the final product might look like from all sides without actually building a physical model. Once designed and programmed into the computer, we can walk or ride through one scene or an entire attraction. If something about the design does not appear to be working, changes can be easily made and tested out with the computer before work begins on the actual model. Models of ride vehicles are also built on the computer, allowing us to view and test all angles of their design and their ability to function as designed—long before we build the genuine article. Computer-modeling was used extensively in the creation of the Indiana Jones Adventure at Disneyland and the Test Track ride at the General Motors pavilion at Epcot.

Another method of modeling that accommodates an even more realistic fully-dimensional view is a large-scale walkthrough model. Built and placed upon shoulder-high supports, these models allow the viewer to be the ride vehicle as they physically step though every detailed scene.

Originally located at the Studio, the model shop moved to WED Enterprises in Glendale in 1960 when work began on the New York World's Fair pavilions and on the Enchanted Tiki Room for Disneyland. Today, Imagineering model shops are located in several buildings, all together encompassing about 80,000 square feet of space.

RIGHT: Imagineer Frank Newman puts the final touches on the scale model of the "Tree of Life," the theme show for Disney's Animal Kingdom. The actual tree will tower 13 stories above the park. Throughout the process of building this model (above), the architects, structural engineers and construction managers would work together with the sculptors to ensure that the tree could be built without compromising its tree-like look.

"The model shop is where the answers are."

—ROLLY CRUMP

ABOVE AND RIGHT: **Detailed exterior and interior models were created to visualize Space Mountain at Disneyland Paris, one of the most complex roller coasters ever built. The interior model allowed the engineers and the designers to understand how the track would interact with the show inside the mountain. The original track model was built using parts from a roller coaster kit purchased at a local toy store—but the pieces for the final model, seen here, were accurate to scale, cut to shape by a computer-controlled laser beam.**

BELOW: In place of the different themed lands that you would find at Disneyland, Tokyo Disney Sea will be made up of seven themed "seas." This finely detailed model enables everyone to envision themselves "inside the park" long before construction actually begins and helps resolve such key issues as architectural styles, color schemes, and even the width of the walkways.

"Last year alone, we made 150 models. We don't save every model we've ever made, because if we did, we'd need 30 buildings just to house them all. But we have stored about 1,700 of those we feel are significant."

—BILL VANEK

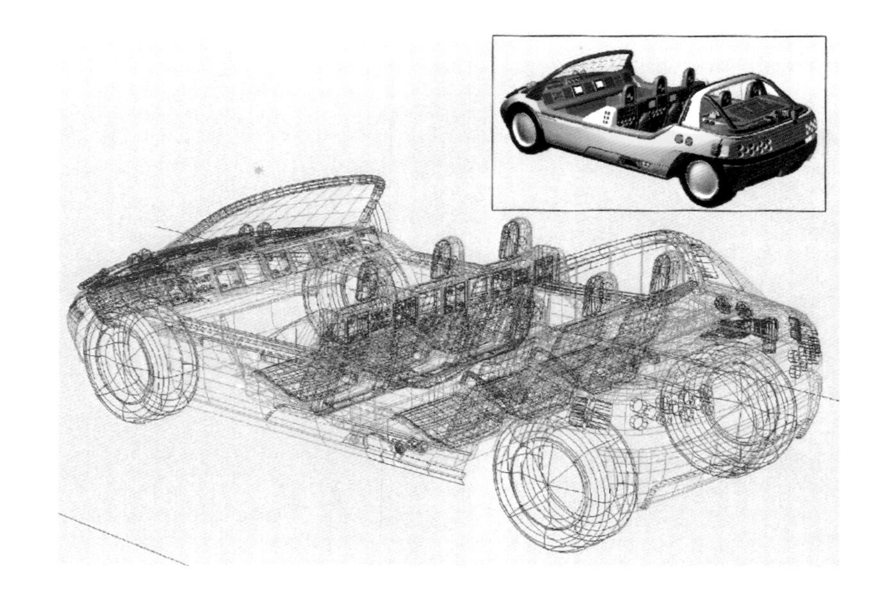

Modeling in Virtual Space

ABOVE: When design began for the Test Track attraction at Epcot, the Imagineers faced one of their most unusual challenges: creating a self-propelled, individually-controlled car that could carry six passengers at freeway speeds on a steeply banked aerial track—traveling more miles in one year than most cars do in five. And they had to design it all in less than nine months. After a lengthy series of design and engineering meetings, the basics were hammered out and Bill Casey drew a felt pen sketch of what the car might look like (above left). Working with this sketch, and incorporating the actual engineering specifications, Albert Yu created an accurate three-dimensional wireframe computer image of the car (above right). This computer image was then sent across the phone lines to Detroit, Michigan, where a computer-operated lathe carved a full-size prototype of the car out of giant blocks of foam. From this prototype the final cars would be built.

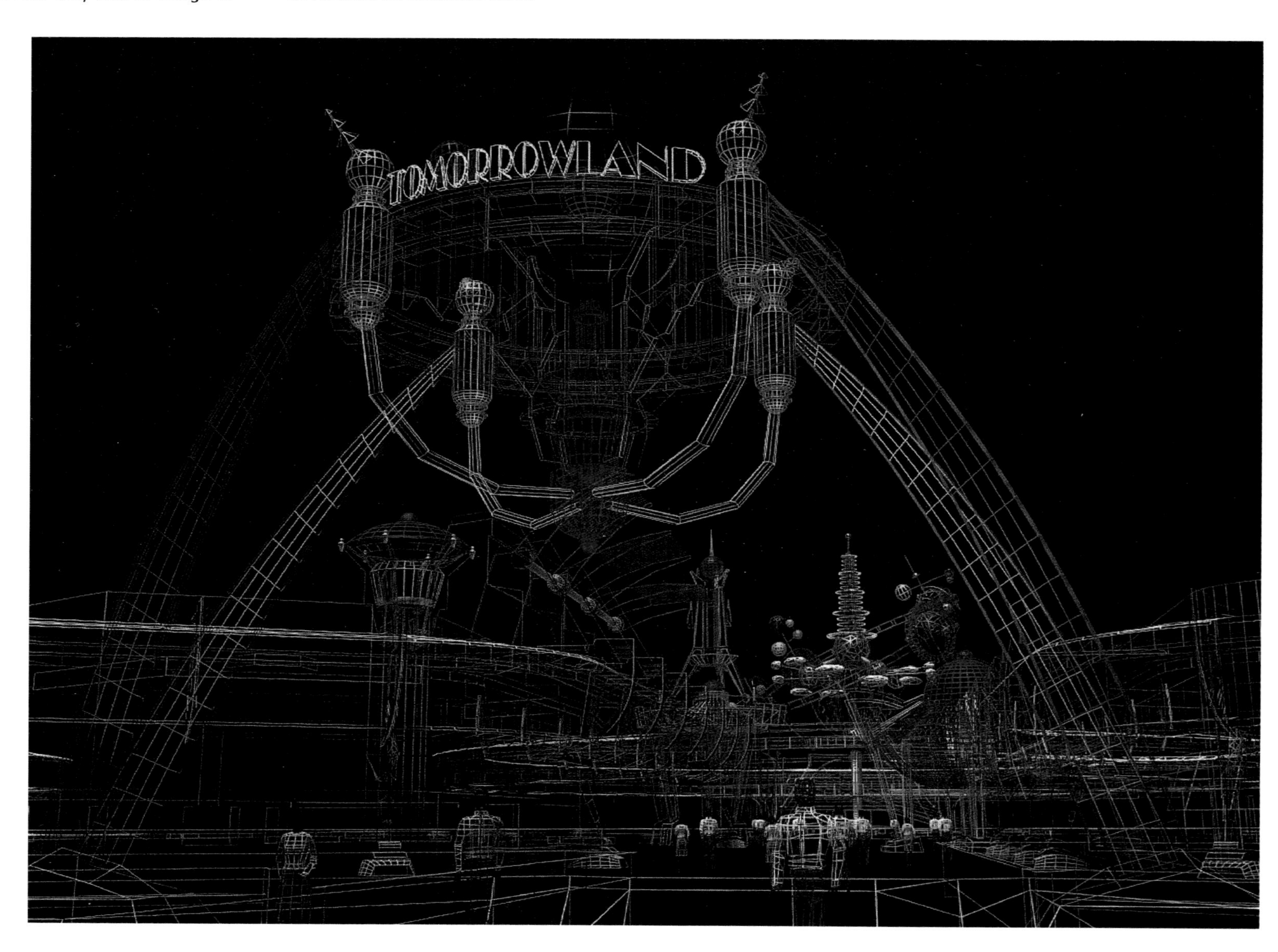

"There are no days in life so memorable as those which vibrate to some stroke of the imagination."

—RALPH WALDO EMERSON

OPPOSITE AND ABOVE: At left, a computer wireframe rendering created in 1994 by Michael Browne, as part of an early study for the New Tomorrowland in the Magic Kingdom at the Walt Disney World Resort. Computer assisted drawings like this one allow the designers to quickly develop architectural shapes, understand their relative sizes and relationships, and easily modify the different elements. Above, color, texture and lighting are added to the wireframe model—all of which can easily be changed as the design evolves. In addition, the computer renderings can be animated, which allows the designers to "walk through" the project at this very early stage of development.

"When I first saw the spirals of Mont Saint-Michel rising up as if out of nowhere, it looked like a mirage. I got goosebumps."

–TOM MORRIS

STEPPING OUT INTO THE WORLD

How do you design and build a fantasy castle on a continent that, for centuries, has boasted the most fantasy-like castles in the world? A good question. And one we had to face when designing Disneyland Paris.

Before he was assigned to the Disneyland Paris project, Imagineer Tom Morris fulfilled a personal dream and went to Europe to photograph castles and picturesque, off-the-beaten-path villages. As luck would have it, when he returned home, he was given the responsibility of designing a new Sleeping Beauty Castle for the European park.

Guided by senior vice president Tony Baxter, executive designer of the park, Tom and artist Brian Jowers set out to create a unique design. The team began by pasting several images of castles they found in books and magazines—both Disney and non-Disney—on a storyboard. They even used sketches and original watercolor studies of the fantasy castles designed by Gustaf Tenggren for the film *Snow White and the Seven Dwarfs,* and those based on early Renaissance paintings by Eyvind Earle for the film *Sleeping Beauty*. Their research revealed that real castles were horizontally oriented for protection against the enemy, but castles in literature and film tended to have a vertical, inspirational orientation.

To top off its design, the Fantasyland team wanted the castle to present a certain element of Frenchness to pay tribute to its new home. Robert Fitzpatrick, then vice president of the EuroDisney project, gave Tom the book *Les Tres Riche Heures* by the Duc de Berri hoping it might serve as cultural inspiration. Its Biblical tales and fables from the 13th and 14th centuries were illustrated through illuminated manuscripts from the period.

After thoroughly researching castles of every kind, it was not a castle at all that helped determine the design in Tom's mind, but a twelfth-century monastery situated on the shore of

TOP: Imagineer Tom Morris sketched this proposal for a fanciful castle, inspired by the Sleeping Beauty styling of Eyvind Earle and a visit to Mont Saint-Michel in France.

LEFT: Working from Tom's sketch, Bryan Jowers created this first rendering of what was to become Le Chateau de la Belle au Bois Dormant, the landmark of Disneyland Paris.

ABOVE: Building a park in France brought with it new challenges in dealing with the very different weather patterns of Europe. This castle rendering is one of a series by Joe Rohde created to explore how a variety of color schemes would look during the different seasons of the year.

OPPOSITE: Concept Designer Tim Delaney proposed this dramatic departure for the centerpiece of Disneyland Paris—an art nouveau-inspired observation tower that would stand as a tribute to great European visionaries such as Jules Verne and H. G. Wells.

ABOVE: **With the design of the castle finally agreed upon, Frank Armitage created this piece of marketing art to help introduce Disneyland Paris to Europe and the world.**

RIGHT: **Guests brave enough to venture down the winding staircase that leads from Merlin's Magic Shop in Fantasyland at Disneyland Paris find themselves deep in the bowels of the castle, face to face with a fire-breathing dragon. Here, Terri Harden puts the finishing touches on the scale model.**

Normandy in Northern France. The towering abbey, Mont Saint-Michel, and its surrounding village fortress are built upon a solid granite island joined to the mainland by a causeway.

For Tom, Mont Saint-Michel, with its staircases like delicate lace spiraling up to heaven, embraced an incredible sense of power, spirituality and fantasy—exactly how the Fantasyland team wanted our guests to feel about Le Chateau de la Belle au Bois Dormant.

Trying to evoke a similar feeling in its design, Tom began to define the shape of the new castle in a pencil sketch. When Tom completed his pencil study of the concept, it was passed along to Imagineering artist Frank Armitage for interpretation into a painting. Ironically, Frank began his career as a background illustrator in the Animation department. He actually painted many of the backgrounds used in the film *Sleeping Beauty*.

Inspired by castles from fantasy and reality, then designed and built with a Disney touch, Le Chateau de la Belle au Bois Dormant stands out from the rest as a very different, very special place.

"Sleeping Beauty Castle at Disneyland was inspired by the Neuschwanstein Castle in Southern Germany. This European influence was fine for building a castle in Anaheim, but the fact that castles exist just down the road from Disneyland Paris challenged us to think twice about our design."

—TONY BAXTER

Still, many are the unknowns as we bring the idea from our first spark to the dawn of the fantasy. For now, our idea remains a restless infant. Before it can mature and grow, blood, sweat, and tears must flow.

ABOVE: The courtyard of Le Chateau de la Belle au Bois Dormant, as seen by Bryan Jowers.

RIGHT: A striking perspective looking down through the interior of Le Chateau de la Belle au Bois Dormant, by artist Bryan Jowers.

CHAPTER 3 # BLOOD, SWEAT AND

"Engineering here is the collision of art and science. It's imagineering."
—BRAN FERREN

Coming up with a wonderful idea for a show or attraction is one thing, but actually building it is quite another. Generally, each idea presents a multitude of design challenges beyond any we have ever experienced. These unknowns force us to employ new ways of thinking and doing—creating new materials or inventing new technologies.

Consider, for example, creating a twenty-passenger elevator that "breaks free from its cable" and drops down a thirteen-story shaft even faster than it possibly could free-fall under the force of gravity—only to ease to a safe stop at the bottom. Or a full-sized airplane that taxis onto an amphitheater stage to explode into a giant inferno, ten times a day, every day of the year. Or a brand new group of buildings that appear as if they are part of the centuries-old streets of Morocco. Or maybe a twelve-passenger boat that takes a death-defying plunge over a roaring waterfall every fifteen seconds—backwards. Or even a nightmarish alien creature that drips hot drool down the back of your neck as it hungrily prepares to claim you for its next victim.

As we invent new technologies to help us realize these concepts, we are not so much concerned about technology for technology's sake as much as we are in using it as a means to tell our story. For us to succeed, the

TEARS

"When we consider a new project, we really study it—not just the surface idea, but everything about it. And when we go into that new project, we believe in it all the way. We have confidence in our ability to do it right. And we work hard to do the best possible job."

—WALT DISNEY

story must be so captivating that the amazing technology supporting it goes completely unnoticed.

Working together, we are a creative melting pot, but working as individual Imagineers, we approach every idea with specific regard to our own fields of expertise. Someone with a talent for theatrical lighting looks at an idea differently than someone who produces special effects. Someone who is well versed in practical building design and construction does not view it in exactly the same way as does the composer of the music that will be heard inside. One Imagineer may know what needs to happen, while another must know how to make it happen.

It takes each and every one of us to make our ideas real. It seldom comes easy. Our process works because as individuals, we approach the idea differently, but together, we share a single vision.

Inspired by the artistic style of Mary Blair, this design was created by artist Paul Hartley exclusively for the "It's a Small World" souvenir book distributed at the 1964 New York World's Fair. The collage featured the tools Imagineers used to create "the happiest cruise that ever sailed around the world."

Standing between what is imagined and what is real, we must reach out to embrace both. The time has come for art and science to unite as one.

Building a Story in Architecture

The first step in translating our dream into reality is to create a building in which it can live. At Disney theme parks, a building is not just a building. It might be a forty-five-foot fishing boat precariously balanced high atop a mountain pinnacle, an ancient Mayan pyramid, a cartoon house for Mickey Mouse, a riverboat, a snack stand buried under a huge avalanche, a towering red rock butte, or even a Tower of Terror.

In Imagineering architecture, the obvious function of a building is secondary to its primary purpose: to help tell the story. Each building's foundation not only supports a physical structure, but it also supports a story structure. Whether facade, mountain, tower, sphere, an entire resort hotel, the wacky neighborhood of Mickey's Toontown, the rustic log structures of Frontierland, the rich-in-detail World Showcase pavilions at Epcot, or the fairytale settings in Fantasyland, Imagineering's approach to architectural storytelling communicates the theme of an entire area.

Imagineers are great observers. We do not confine ourselves to the worlds of fantasy we create within our theme parks, but rather, learn much of what we do from careful scrutiny of the world outside our park perimeters. The architectural evolution of most major cities is the result of a series of accidental layers, things building upon other things without thoughtful arrangement. In many instances, this creates a lack of order, which, in turn, creates visual conflict. By understanding what does not work, we can eliminate visual conflict and contradiction in what we create. In doing so, we can provide an environment that is pleasant, friendly and reassuring.

At the Disney theme parks, each architectural environment invites a specific reaction. Along the non-threatening turn-of-the-century Main Street, U.S.A., guests become members of an interactive community, where they even talk to strangers. The environment contributes to their openness, and people who would never speak with a stranger in their own home towns mingle freely.

Main Street is also a prime spot to see "forced perspective," the art of making something appear taller than it actually is. With its roots in motion pictures, forced perspective is accomplished architecturally by starting with normal scale elements at the base of a building and progressively making them smaller as they continue towards the top. Sleeping Beauty Castle and the facades on Main Street are normal size at ground level, smaller at the second level, still smaller above that, and so on. Even the trees in the area are trimmed so as not to grow out of scale.

Surprisingly, the shared opinion among renowned architects soon after Disneyland opened was that most of the park's buildings were nothing more than "fake" studio facades. Architect Charles Moore radically broke from this mainstream thinking when he wrote the following in *The City Observed: Los Angeles*:

People often use Disneyland as a synonym for the facile, shallow and fake. It just doesn't wash: This incredibly energetic collection of environmental experiences offers enough lessons for a whole architectural education in all the things that matter—community and reality, private memory and inhabitation, as well as technical lessons in propinquity and choreography.

Imagineered buildings are not simple structures or studio facades, but whole events. They are the illustrated book covers leading to the stories that await inside. Creating a sense of time, place and mood, Imagineered architecture can, in a single instant, transport you to a distant land.

"Much of Fantasyland was architecturally designed to lean, slope and have that 'caved-in' storybook appearance. When the contractor came on board to frame the buildings, we found that because he was not used to building things that are crooked, he proceeded to frame them straight to 'correct' our 'mistakes.' After a few weeks of Disney orientation, he was finally able to embellish our intent."

—DAVID VAN WYK

OPPOSITE: Depicting the south elevation of the eighteen-story-high Cinderella Castle at the Magic Kingdom at Walt Disney World, this detailed architectural drawing created under the direction of Bill Martin represents the first step in turning an artist's concept into a reality.

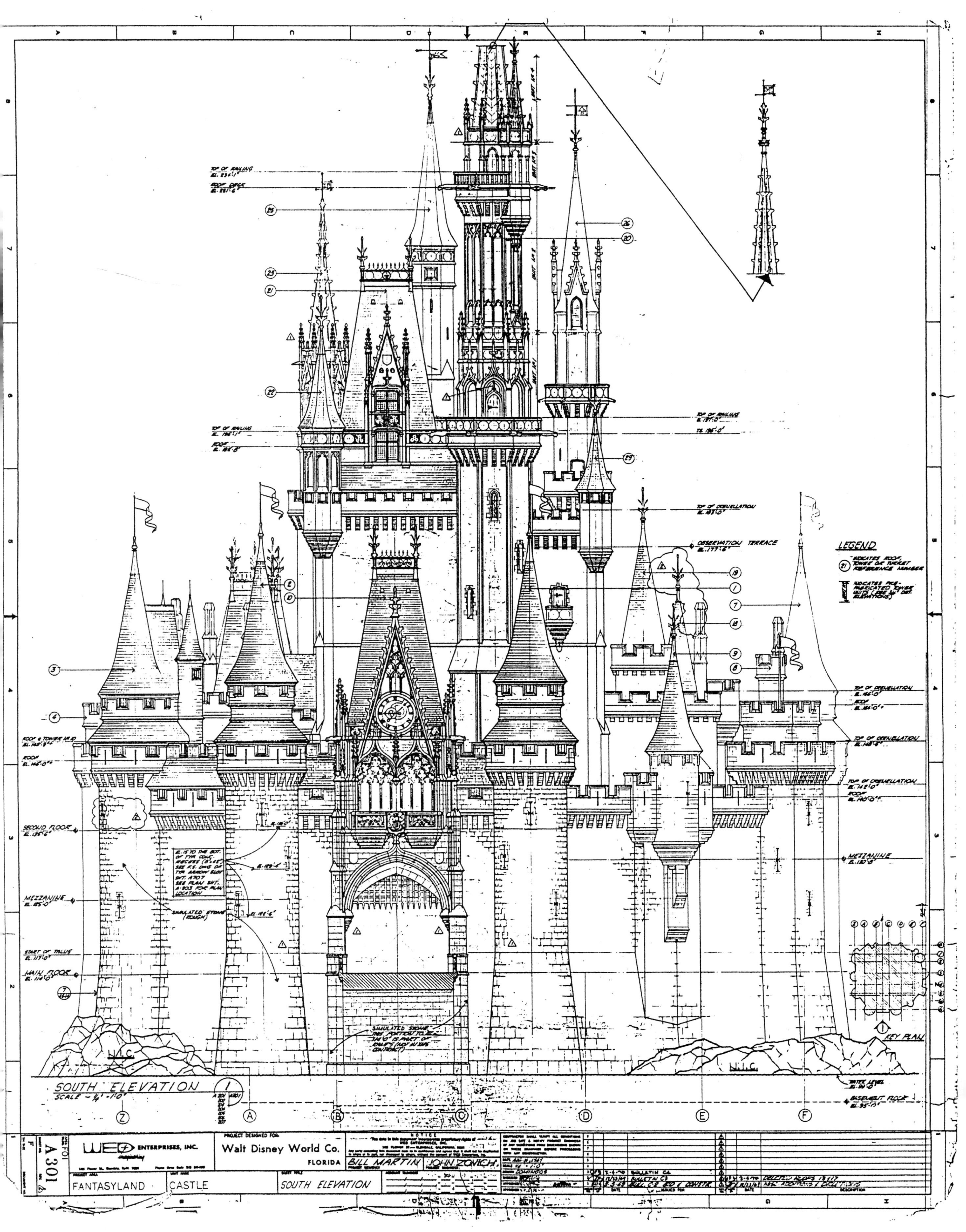

SOUTH ELEVATION
SCALE - 1/8" = 1'-0"
LEGEND
KEY PLAN
OBSERVATION TERRACE
SECOND FLOOR
MEZZANINE
MAIN FLOOR
START OF TALUS
BASEMENT FLOOR
WATER LEVEL
SIMULATED STONE (ROUGH)
WED ENTERPRISES, INC.
PROJECT DESIGNED FOR:
Walt Disney World Co.
FLORIDA
BILL MARTIN
JOHN ZOVICH
FANTASYLAND
CASTLE
SOUTH ELEVATION
A 301

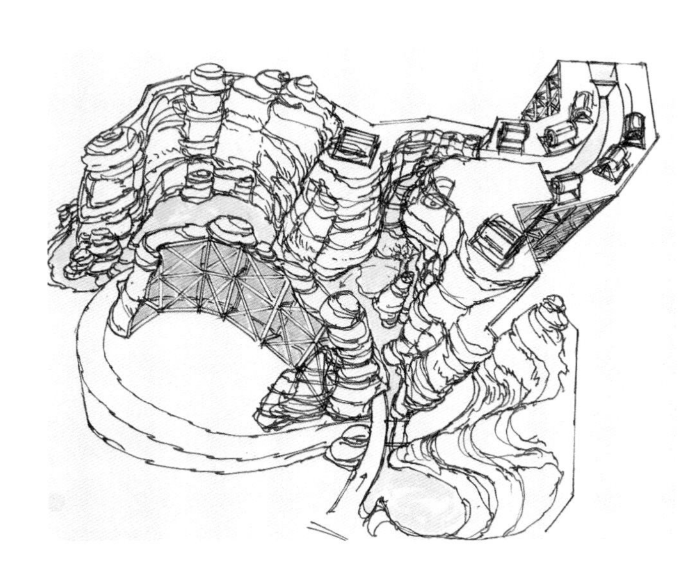

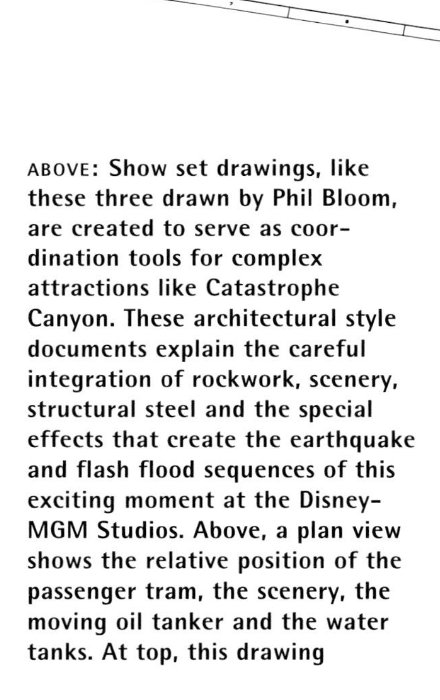

Engineering Dreams into Reality

Somewhere between dreaming what we want and building what we'll get lies one of the strongest elements of our team dynamic: engineering. (Think of it as the "engine" that pulled up the "eering" to the "imagine" part of our name.)

At Imagineering, engineering means translating one-of-a-kind ideas into buildable realities. Meeting this tremendous challenge and ensuring that Imagineering has or makes the tools necessary to produce the world's best and most unique entertainment experiences are the mission of engineers at Imagineering.

Imagineers whose field of expertise is engineering, whether electrical, civil, structural or mechanical, are not just the most creative engineers in the world, but are among the most creative people in the world. They have the ability to dream with the dreamers and build with the builders. Their creative solutions to supposed impossibilities can't be found in any how-to book.

All of the projects we create, because they are one-of-a-kind in nature, are heavily burdened with one-of-a-kind unknowns. At Catastrophe Canyon, located along the Disney–MGM Studios tram tour, a tram-shaking earthquake occurs every four minutes, causing a full-sized oil tanker truck to explode into a fiery inferno. Then, along with 70,000 gallons of water gushing from a flash flood and a broken water tower, the truck slides down the canyon walls towards the shaking, water-engulfed tram. All this resets to explode again for the next tram in less than four minutes. Solutions to make the impossible possible are discovered every day at Imagineering.

That's why, as soon as the spark of an idea catches fire, a concept team recruits one or more of our engineers to contribute to the initial brainstormings and subsequent concept development.

Ultimately, no matter how incredible an idea may be, it will always remain just an idea until every design challenge has a practical solution and drawings are precise enough that they can be handed to someone who can build from them. Engineers are the ones who will eventually have to figure out exactly how the dream can be turned into reality.

ABOVE: Show set drawings, like these three drawn by Phil Bloom, are created to serve as coordination tools for complex attractions like Catastrophe Canyon. These architectural style documents explain the careful integration of rockwork, scenery, structural steel and the special effects that create the earthquake and flash flood sequences of this exciting moment at the Disney–MGM Studios. Above, a plan view shows the relative position of the passenger tram, the scenery, the moving oil tanker and the water tanks. At top, this drawing indicates the location of the "shaker tables" that simulate the motion of the earthquake. At opposite top, a detail sheet defines the safety handrail, which must be carefully themed as not to block the view or destroy the believability of the sequence.

ABOVE LEFT: This 1987 concept sketch was the first illustration created to show how the tram vehicle would enter Catastrophe Canyon, and where the special effects water tanks might be located.

"Despite the tremendous odds against us, we always seem to figure out how to make it work. You just have to be optimistic by nature."

—BRUCE JOHNSON

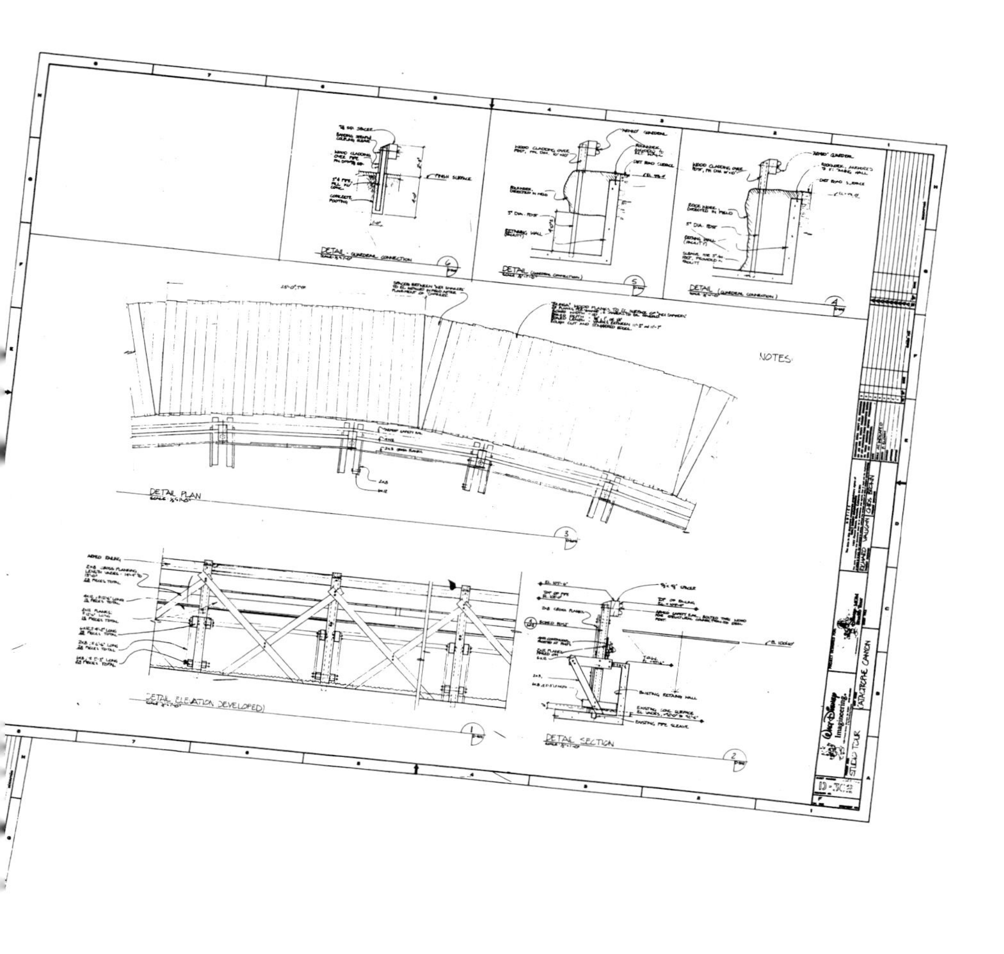

"Engineers everywhere are problem solvers. In this respect, we are no different than outside engineering firms that design and build complex projects like oil refineries. But at Imagineering, there's something about the nature of what we do and our unique product that makes our jobs more challenging, interesting and fun."

—ART HENDERSON

BELOW: "Catastrophe" strikes when all the designs come together and 70,000 gallons of water are released from the giant special effects storage tanks, narrowly avoiding the tram-load of guests watching from below.

"Architecturally speaking, what I do at Imagineering is more important and more powerful than anything I could ever accomplish in a conventional realm. I feel that what we have already done pales in comparison to what we are about to do."

—CHRIS CARRADINE

ABOVE: This concept rendering by Group West relies upon familiar Italian landmarks, such as Doge's Palace and the Campanile, or bell tower, to capture the essence of a leisurely stroll through an Italian piazza. Those who are familiar with the original Venetian buildings, however, will notice that this World Showcase arrangement is reversed. No, the negative wasn't printed backwards. Bill Martin arranged the landmarks this way so as not to do a "cold copy" of the originals. He felt that this way, the Italy pavilion could enjoy its own unique identity.

BELOW LEFT: This site plan of the Italy pavilion displays the arrangement of the individual architectural elements, as well as showing how the entire layout fits into the grand scheme of World Showcase.

BELOW RIGHT: Architectural color elevations, such as this one created by Susan McCauley for the Doge's Palace at the Italy pavilion, establish accurate color palettes from which actual buildings derive their final color schemes. Color elevations are often taken to the field during the construction phase for handy reference.

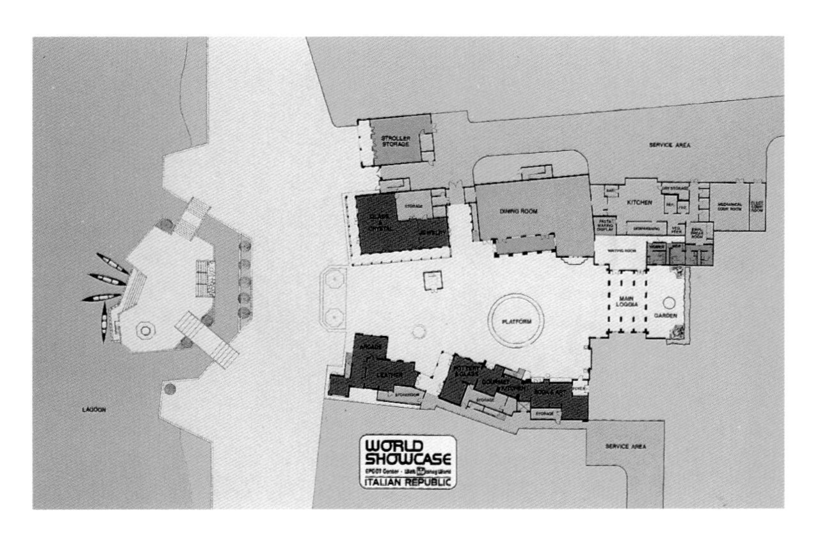

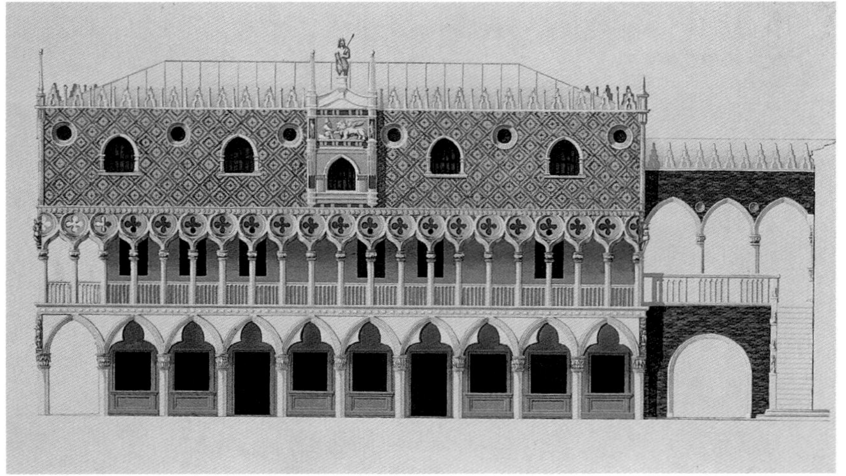

"I don't believe in going to this extreme blue sky stuff that some of the architects do. I believe people still want to live like human beings."

—WALT DISNEY

ABOVE: This interior design by Dorothea Redmond became the Il Bel Cristallo shop at Italy in World Showcase. This type of interior rendering is based upon an architectural drawing—or footprint—that defines the layout and dimensions of the floor space. Given these dimensions, the rendering defines the space, in this case, a shop, by establishing its interior design and mood long before it is built. This also creates a visual menu from which individual interior appointments, such as lighting fixtures, floor and wall coverings and furnishings can be purchased or fabricated in time for installation.

ABOVE RIGHT: At almost all of our theme parks, many of the finely-detailed architectural elements are simulated in foam, fiberglass, wood, and even stamped concrete to accurately represent the original inspiration, whether it be a concept drawing, painting, or actual place or object.

RIGHT: Since most of our projects arrive on site complete with easy-to-follow assembly instructions, there are rarely any parts left over.

If we are to take the idea any further, we must prepare ourselves for a road never traveled. We know not of the challenges that await around all the unexplored twists and turns that lie ahead. Each step forward may mean three steps back. But three steps back reveals our true direction.

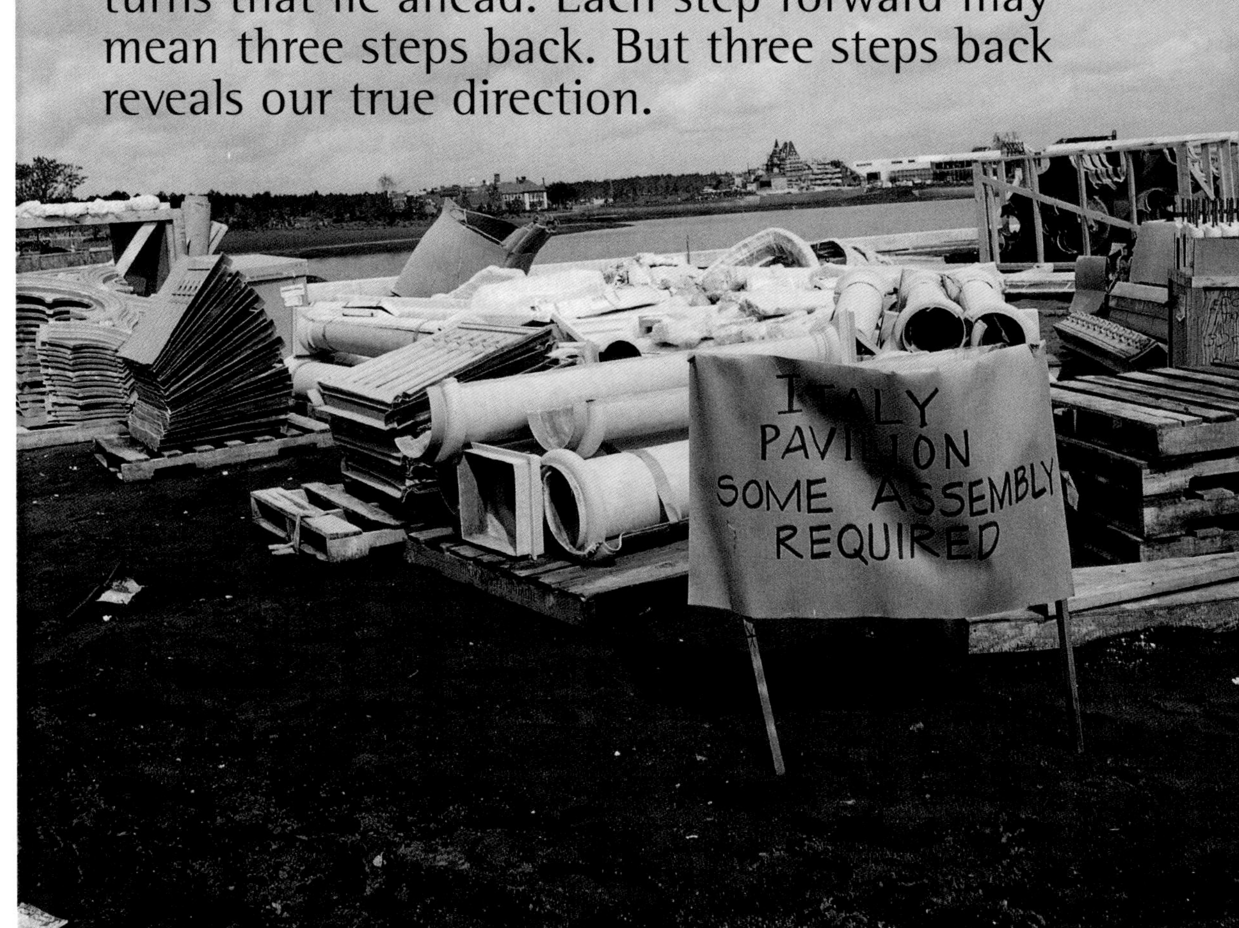

"I don't want the public to see the world they live in while they're in the park. I want them to feel they're in another world."

—WALT DISNEY

A SENSE OF STAGING

Once we have a workable idea that can live in a unique Disney-style building, it is time to put on the show. First, we draw from a seasoned Disney tradition—a strong sense of staging.

Instinctively, Walt Disney understood the communicative power of simplicity. He built the foundation of his company on visual story-telling. When he and Ub Iwerks started making motion pictures in the 1920s, they wanted to tell a complete story in their eight minutes or less of film time. To accomplish this, nothing could interfere with or stray from the idea or action they wished to communicate. Walt had a specific reason for doing everything he did.

When it came time to enter the three-dimensional world of entertainment, he brought the things he learned from film making to creating parks. A motion picture director has the luxury of creating an optical target—by placing action and focus or color. In a theme park, however, the viewer is not just an observer, but a participant. The imagery is not confined to the parameters of a movie screen, and the participant is bombarded with visual overload. The key to making this work is for each element to mesh with the story. When inventing the process of theme park design, Walt and his movie-makers-turned-Imagineers converted many of their film-making principles into three-dimensional application.

One such principle is the cross-dissolve. A stroll from Main Street to Adventureland is a relatively short distance, but one experiences an enormous change in theme and story. For the transition to be a smooth one, there is a gradual blending of themed foliage, color, sound, music and architecture. Even the soles of your feet feel a change in the paving that explicitly tells you something new is on the horizon. Smell may also factor into a dimensional cross-dissolve. In a warm summer breeze, you may catch a whiff of sweet tropical flora and exotic spices as you enter Adventureland. Once all these changes are experienced, the cross-dissolve transition is complete.

ABOVE: In this 1966 concept sketch, designer Claude Coats sets the stage for Pirates of the Caribbean, creating a fitting environment for Mark Davis' pirate characters.

BELOW: All of the many books about pirates from our Imagineering research library contain check-out cards filled with Marc Davis' signature. Inspired by his many hours of researching the trouble-some antics of real pirates, Marc was able to turn them into comical situations for the "wildest crew that ever sacked the Spanish Main."

ABOVE: Relying upon what he had learned as a background artist in the studio's animation department, Claude Coats created this one of many models to set the stage for the Pirates of the Caribbean, which opened at Disneyland in 1967. The challenge was to create a theatrical environment for an attraction, which meant that not just one but many scenes had to be connected together to work from an all-around perspective. In like manner, studio animator-turned-Imagineer Marc Davis drew from his years of creating action on film to creating the action that the characters would provide inside the dimensional sets. Both Claude and Marc found their jobs at Imagineering were essentially the same as they had been at the studio, the only difference being they were designing for this side of the silver screen.

"Virtual Reality is basically nothing new. We have been creating Virtual Reality around here for more than forty years."

—JOHN HENCH, Senior Vice President

LEFT: Dozens of Marc Davis' characters created during the concept development of Pirates of the Caribbean never made it beyond a preliminary sketch. But these townspeople were "bound" to end up in model form (above) and eventually, in the attraction itself.

ABOVE: Walt asked one of the "nine old men," animator Marc Davis (left) and animator-turned-sculptor Blaine Gibson (right) to join Imagineering to continue doing what they had been doing for years on film—creating animated characters, but now in three dimensions. (One thing about Marc—he always stood by his characters.)

SETTING THE STAGE . . .

LEFT: Walt Disney convinced General Electric that his Imagineers could produce a unique show that would "showcase the electrical industry and tell how it has helped the nation grow and prosper" for the 1964–1965 New York World's Fair. To sell G.E. on the idea for Progressland, concept renderings of the pavilion and its innovative new show called Walt Disney's Carousel of Progress were assembled on a sequence of storyboards.

LEFT: Sam McKim created this illustration to show how Audio-Animatronics performers would be placed within the stage setting of Act I, as well as highlighting the "animated" roles each would play.

BELOW: Since Walt Disney's Carousel of Progress was the first "live" stage show ever to employ a cast made up entirely of Audio-Animatronics performers, special consideration had to be given to the stage setting and the character and prop placement. This was Sam McKim's original stage concept proposed for Act II. It not only set the scene, but displayed how the characters would be staged to allow close access to their behind-the-scenes support equipment.

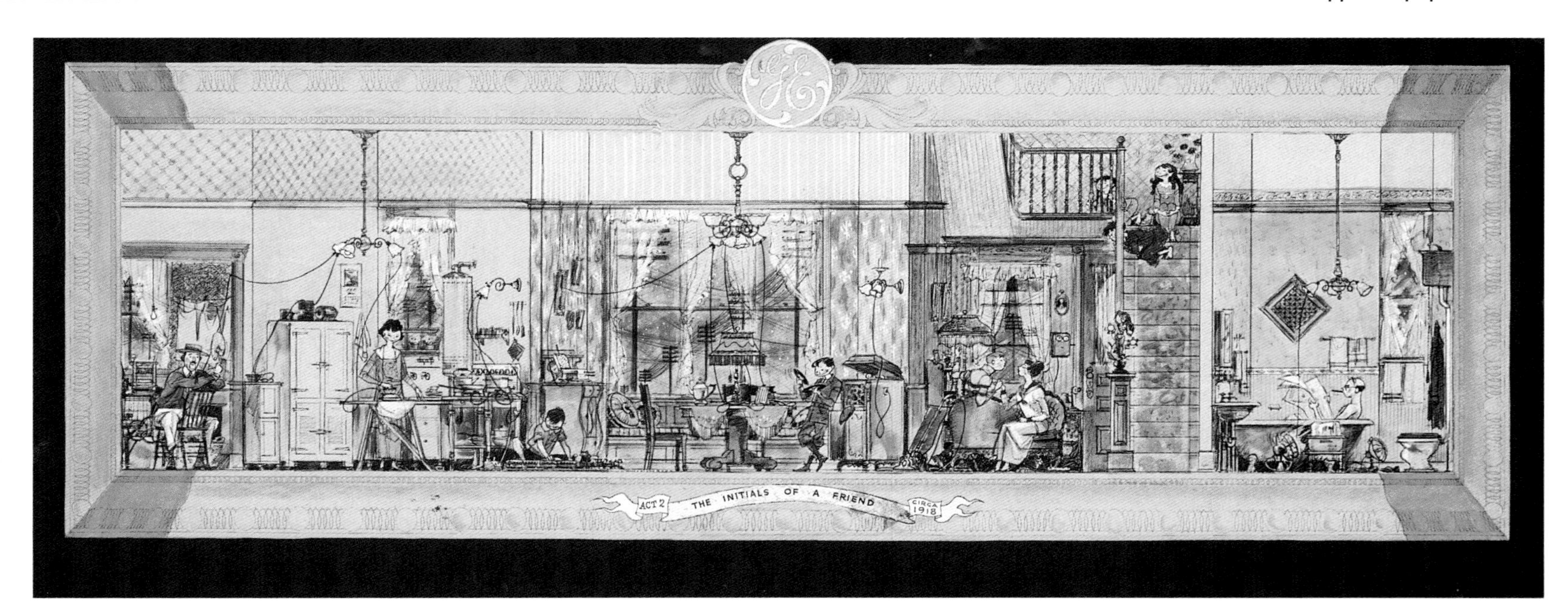

LEFT: To prove it would operate as designed before being shipped to New York, a "mock-up" of the entire show was assembled and filmed on a soundstage at the Disney Studio in Burbank. The film was sent to General Electric as a "work-in-progress," and was later shown as part of "Disneyland Goes to the World's Fair," a special episode of the *Wonderful World of Color* television show which aired on May 17, 1964.

BELOW LEFT: Marc Davis was handed the task of coming up with gag situations for the performers—each gag, of course, having to do with how electricity made life better. After Marc created this scene for "Cousin Orville" as he would appear in Act II, Walt commented that Orville's toes should be sticking out over the top of the tub. "And," added Walt, "they should be wiggling!"

BELOW RIGHT: Here is Cousin Orville, complete with wiggling toes, as he appeared at the fair. Mel Blanc, renowned for his character voices at Warner Brothers Studios, moonlighted one day in 1963 to provide the voice for the character. This was the only show Mel ever did for Disney other than giving the cavemen in the Ford Pavilion their grunts. Prior to recording Orville's voice, Mel was told that the character would be smoking a cigar. So Mel "smoked" a pencil during the recording session to add that extra touch of reality.

BELOW: This concept design turned the Carousel into the future for the final act. While John Hench was predicting the design of the post-1960s American living room, he probably would have been amazed to learn that, because the attraction would be so successful over the years, his set design would be updated several times to keep up with real progress. Walt Disney's Carousel of Progress would eventually be seen by more audiences than any other show in the history of American Theater. Even though the show has been changed over the years, the Carousel, now at the Magic Kingdom at Walt Disney World, still revolves around the same theme—progress.

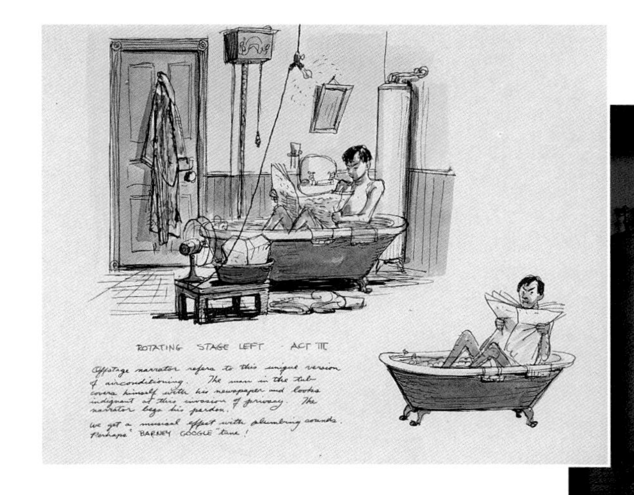

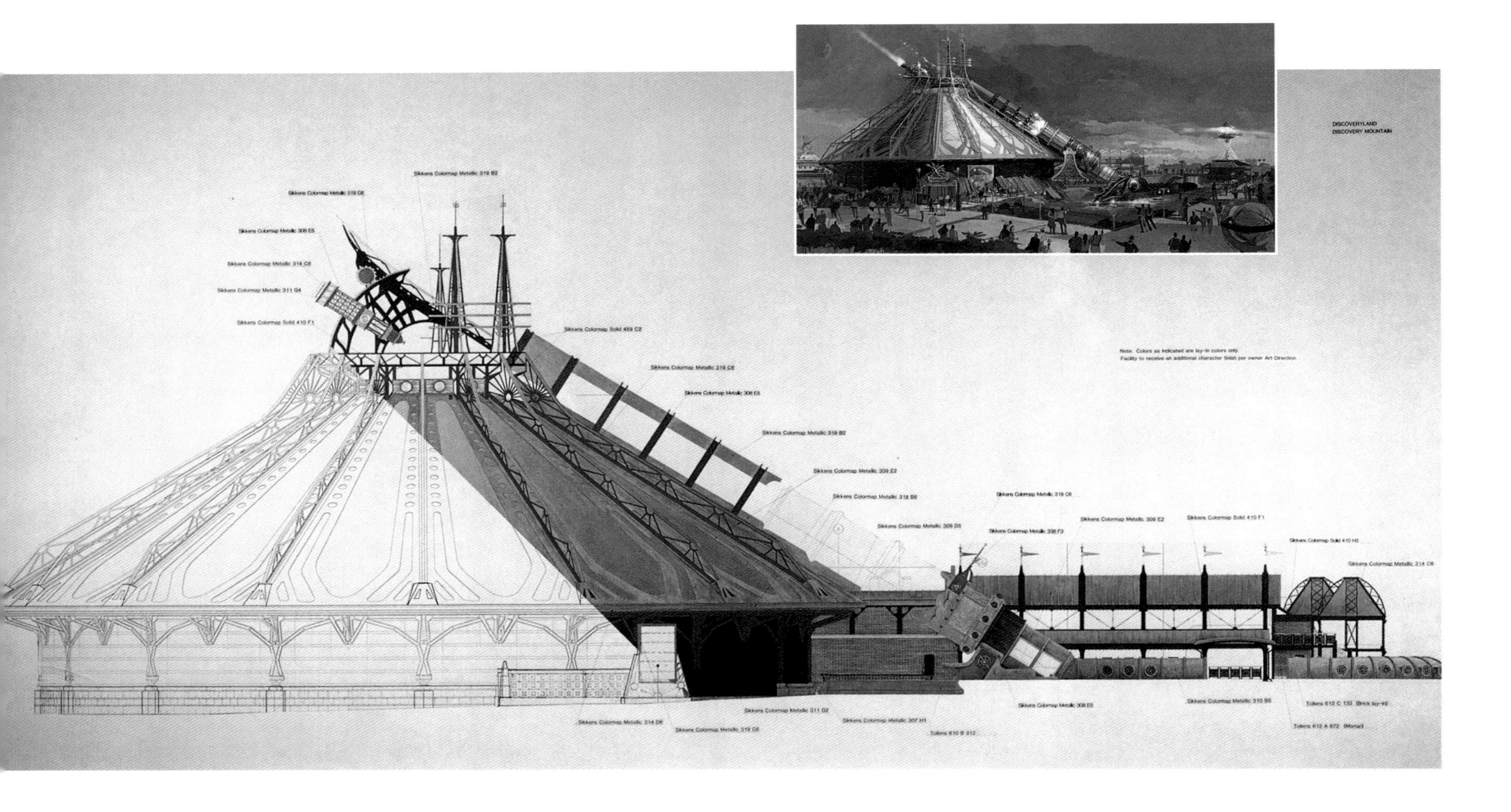

WONDERFUL WORLD OF COLOR

TOP: **In many cases, the color scheme that appears in the early concept renderings, such as this one painted by Tim Delaney for Space Mountain in Disneyland Paris, turns out to be the final choice for the completed attraction.**

ABOVE: **Before construction or production of a project even begins, "color boards" are created to reflect every aspect of the intended color overlay. The first type is an "elevation" color board, upon which an artist paints the intended exterior color scheme directly onto architectural elevation drawings. The color scheme for the board shown at the top, painted by Katie Olson, was derived from Tim Delaney's original concept rendering above. Attached to an architectural color board are paint chips and samples of other exterior treatments, such as gold leafing, brick or tile, with their intended designation indicated on the drawing. The second type of board reflects the colors and patterns chosen for the interior treatments specifically, which includes an assembly of paint chips, swatches and samples for furnishings and wall and floor coverings. Once completed and approved, these boards become the color vocabulary for the entire project.**

"Where there is color," says Imagineering senior vice president John Hench, "there is life!" We can hardly address the topic of color in this book without considering John Hench's philosophy, thoughtful study and seasoned knowledge about the subject. Indeed, if you have been to any one or all of the Disney parks, you have seen and experienced his touch of magic. As well as being a legendary Disney studio artist and theme park designer, John has been the quintessential resident color expert at Imagineering since the day Walt established the company. He has been with Disney for over 56 years. And we still draw from his wisdom.

"We humans have an intimate relationship with color, having to do with the 100,000 year old memories we cart around with us," John adds. "Color is one of those mysterious elements that awakens our basic survival instinct. Certain colors are reassuring, while others imply action. All of them deliver messages. For early man, the reappearing color of springtime always meant the return of food, such as fruits, vegetables, and the fresh red meat of game. If you want someone to look at something specific in a film or painting, make it red."

While experimenting with color, scientists communicated with primitive tribes through interpreters, asking them to pick a handful of favorites from among several color swatches. When choosing from among the non-primary colored swatches, such as several shades of violet, their selections were entirely different than those chosen by modern humans. But when they selected from among all the shades of primary colors, their choices were exactly the same. These were blood red, sky blue, and foliage green - colors basic to all human beings.

According to John, humans respond to color both consciously, and subconsciously. Any conflict of order, including disregard for the effective application of color, can affect our instincts and sense of balance.

In addition, the Imagineering colorist must be sensitive to natural lighting from a global perspective. "Depending upon where you are in the world," adds John, "the quality of light and the intensity of the sun varies. This has a major impact on the choice and application of color. The light is different in Orlando than in Anaheim, and in Paris it differs from both. Light in Paris, however, is similar to Tokyo. It all boils down to this: if improperly applied at our theme parks, color could negatively impact our guest's experience. And they may not even know why."

It is no coincidence, then, that Imagineers have tremendous respect for the abilities and power of color. Rarely do we paint something a particular color simply because it looks nice. Careful consideration goes into each selection, no matter how small the application.

Behind every color used in our projects lies an important reason for its use. In fact, influenced by John Hench, we have created an entire color vocabulary at Imagineering, which includes colors and patterns we have found that stir basic human instincts—including that of survival. We draw from that vocabulary for use in our projects to provide calmness and gentle reassurance where appropriate. Or if a scene requires conflict to effect mood, color is used to play that role as well.

RIGHT AND BELOW: **The identity, theme and texture of an architectural element often take form first in a black and white pencil sketch, as is apparent in this scene from Frontierland by artist Sam McKim. Once color is added, the scene comes to life.**

The color process begins with an initial concept rendering that defines the big idea, followed by more paintings that identify the major elements found inside. Amazingly, sometimes these concept illustrations are extremely accurate in predicting the color future of the project.

Before Imagineering illustrator Nina Rae Vaughn begins a painting that depicts a project idea, she paints a series of rough "color studies." These allow her to experiment freely with splashes of color, while at the same time, blocking out the basic shape of the concept. Once she has "visually organized her thoughts," she will choose her favorite study as a guide for the colors she will use in the final detailed rendering.

"Different projects call for different uses of color," says Nina. "If a project wants to communicate 'fun', like Mickey's Toontown, I will experiment with bright colors, applying the brightest of brights against the darkest of darks. If the idea says 'adventure,' like the Indiana Jones Adventure, I will use colors that shout action and excitement. These are hot reds and oranges, with shadows of complimentary colors like blues, that make the hot colors even more vibrant."

The master Imagineering artists that made the transition from the studio to WED, like John Hench and Herbert Ryman, were instrumental in nurturing the next generation of in-house talent by passing along their expertise and color philosophies to artists like Nina. "One day I was doing a color study for the interior of a china shop for Disneyland Paris," recalls Nina. "I was applying subtle colors and pastels with tiny brushes to try to create a sense of elegance. Herbie came in to my office and asked if I wouldn't mind if he painted on my painting. I said of course not, and he picked out the biggest watercolor brush I had, saturated it in pure red pigment, and painted a straight line all the way across the board. 'There,' he said. 'That's the velvet that the china sits on!' Herbie taught me not to be afraid of color. He really opened my eyes!" Nina keeps that study directly above her drawing board to remind her of the communicative power of color.

In concert with every other element, the colors we select for our parks help identify and compliment each story and theme, while adding to the quality of the action. When Disneyland was opened, the introduction of guests into the environment created a new dynamic which had an impact on some of the colors used. To be certain all of the colors would work well with the new action occurring on the "scene," Walt sent John Hench to the park twice a month to identify possible color problems and to make adjustments accordingly. Some of the changes were quite subtle, but they were made nonetheless. "To complement the action on Main Street," remembers John, "we introduced a more saturate color throughout. It was an appropriate and stimulating response to the attitude and feeling of the guests. It just seemed to give the place more life."

"To be sure all of the colors would work well with the new action occurring on the scene, Walt would send us to the park twice a month to identify possible color problems and to make adjustments accordingly. Some of the changes were quite subtle, but they were made nonetheless."

—JOHN HENCH

Department of the Interiors

At Imagineering, interior design takes on a whole new meaning. It helps tell the story of a ride, attraction, shop or restaurant. The interior design shop provides handy access to hundreds of catalogs and countless samples of fabric swatches, tiles, wallcoverings, draperies, flooring and many other materials.

If a project requires an object, material, or treatment we do not have readily available, we will search near and far for it. Or we will create it ourselves, whether it be carpet, wall or window coverings, light fixtures, furniture—just about anything.

ABOVE AND RIGHT: One of the challenges Ruben Viramontes had while designing the Adventureland Bazaar at Disneyland Paris was that the indoor shop was supposed to look like an outdoor street scene. When the facility was built—as suggested in the concept sketch above—a false roof was placed in front of a structural skylight so natural outdoor light could filter down to the "street."

ABOVE: Kathleen Charles and Ruben Viramontes are creating interior treatment samples for the Adventureland Bazaar. Samples like these are then attached to "color sample boards"—the reference palette from which the interior materials are purchased and fabricated for installation in the field.

BELOW: These color sample boards for the Adventureland Bazaar display actual samples of the interior treatments selected or fabricated for purchase and eventual installation. Note the attached leaves, wall textures, cabinet hardware, and even a lashed-together wood sample from which a wooden camel would be fabricated.

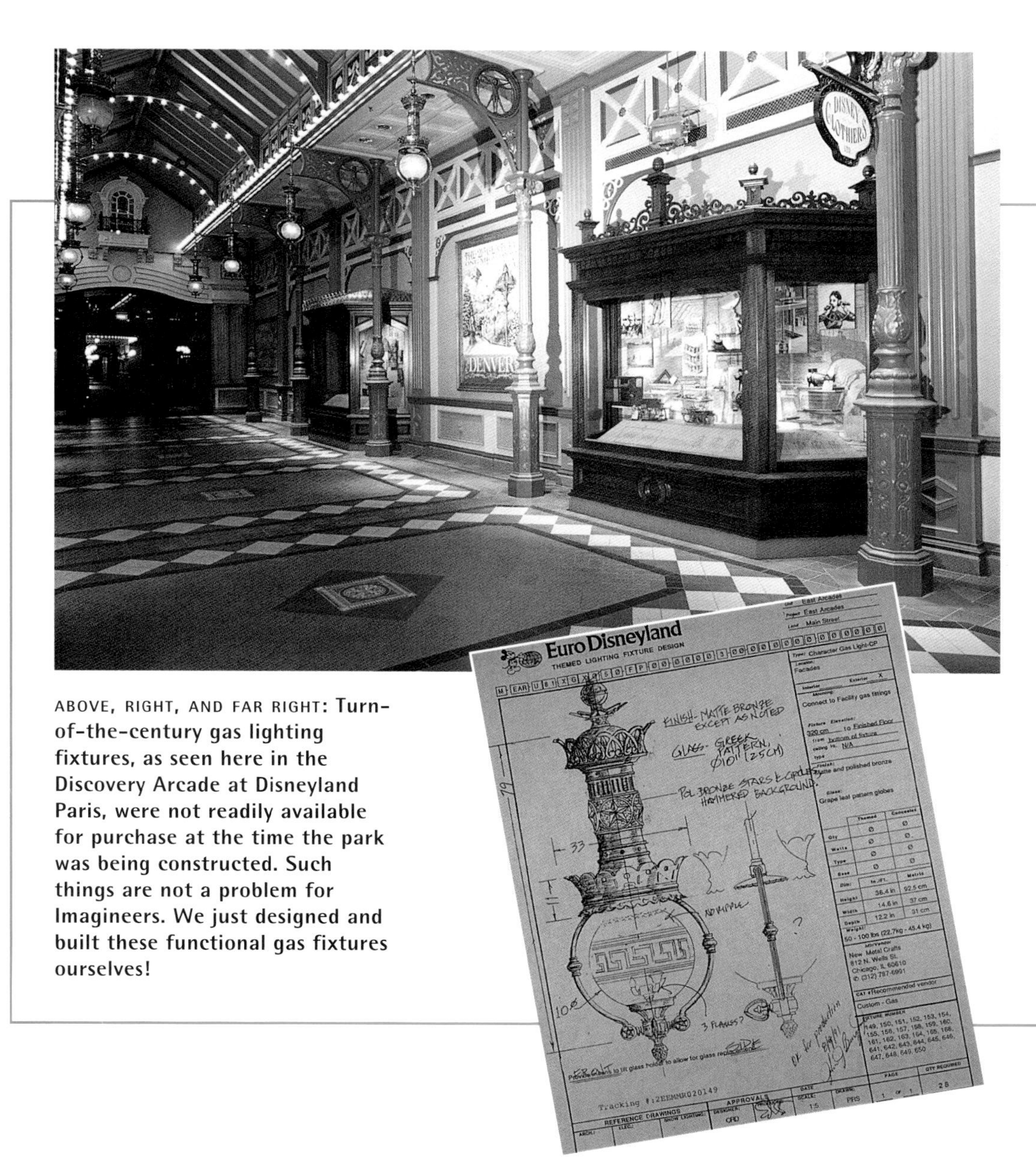

ABOVE, RIGHT, AND FAR RIGHT: **Turn-of-the-century gas lighting fixtures, as seen here in the Discovery Arcade at Disneyland Paris, were not readily available for purchase at the time the park was being constructed. Such things are not a problem for Imagineers. We just designed and built these functional gas fixtures ourselves!**

ABOVE AND RIGHT: **During the concept development phase of Disneyland Paris, Nina Rae Vaughn illustrated how "Casey's Corner" Restaurant might appear on Main Street. As suggested to her by the interior design team, Nina filled the space with early American memorabilia. Once it was built, the restaurant clearly reflected the original design intent.**

Creating new ideas means creating new ways of thinking, conceiving, proceeding, believing. In place of a guess, we believe in trial and error, which soon becomes trial and success.

LEFT: In Nina Rae Vaughn's first concept rendering of the Sci-Fi Dine-In Restaurant for the Disney-MGM Studios, what appears to be an outdoor scene is actually an interior design. The restaurant was designed to be located inside a soundstage-type facility. This piece illustrates how guests could enjoy a drive-in movie on a pleasant summer evening no matter what the actual weather or time of day outside.

BACKGROUND: This cut-away drawing by vehicle designer Bill Casey illustrates how restaurant tables and seats work within a '50s-style car interior.

TURNING THE TABLES ON DESIGN

Custom design and fabrication are more the rule than the exception, especially when you consider interior spaces for something cartoony (like Goofy's Bounce House), elegant (like our replica of Hollywood's Brown Derby Restaurant), scary (like the Haunted Mansion), or period (like a 1950s-style carhop-service drive-in theater restaurant complete with classic convertible cars).

The Sci-Fi Dine-In Theater Restaurant at the Disney–MGM Studios is an example of the untypical way we do interior spaces. The idea was to create a stylized drive-in movie theater reminiscent of the legendary outdoor theaters of the 1950s. With car-side service provided by roller-skating waiters, guests could sit in their cars and watch cartoons and trailers from '50s B-movie science fiction thrillers while enjoying their meal—all in an interior space that seems like an exterior space. Our first design question was, should we make a car that is a table, or make a table that is a car?

The interior designers went to work researching the exterior paint colors and features of the automobiles of that era with the intent of creating small-scale versions for use in the restaurant. For their auto upholstery selection, they actually tracked down a source in Detroit that carried "New Old Stock," an auto restorer's term for goods that are vintage, but brand new in condition (the fabrics actually came with certificates of authenticity). But the cars themselves had to be created from scratch, so our interior designers worked side-by-side with our ride vehicle designers to develop the "convertables." Once designed, they were hand-built at Imagineering by our plastics group from the Mechanical Manufacturing Department.

When the cars were finished, they were delivered to the site and installed facing a drive-in movie screen, then surrounded by panoramic murals depicting the Hollywood Hills at night. The facility roof above them was hidden by a canopy of twinkling summer stars.

Since there are so few drive-in theaters in existence today, many young people have never watched a movie from the familiar comfort of the family car. But at the Sci-Fi Dine-In, a whole new generation can enjoy the taste of a classic burger and a shake as they catch a sci-fi flick from the Fabulous Fifties.

"Even though the Sci-Fi Dine-In was designed as a restaurant first and an attraction second, it's sometimes hard to set them apart."

—ERIC JACOBSON

BELOW: In the Sci-Fi Dine-In Restaurant at the Disney-MGM Studios in Florida, it is always Saturday night in 1956. The perfect summer sky is always filled with stars and the drive-in is always filled with cars. And no need to wait for intermission—the snack bar is always open!

ABOVE RIGHT: Bill Casey's early concept design combined the styling of a classic '50s convertible with restaurant tables, thus creating the world's first and only "conver-table."

ABOVE: Mike Uetz (in front), Darrell Payne and Ed Pendleton (in background), of the MAPO plastics shop, add the finishing touches to one of 34 "custom" cars they manufactured for a permanent parking place at the Sci-Fi Dine-In Restaurant.

BELOW: Only at Imagineering would automotive designers work side-by-side with interior designers to create a restaurant table that captures the design essence of a car. From an interior designer's perspective, these are cars designed to be tables. From the automotive designer's perspective, these are tables designed to be cars.

"After the restaurant was opened, I heard on two different occasions guests reminiscing about when their folks brought home a new two-tone, chrome-lined car just like the one they were sitting in; or, as teenagers, getting one as their first car. I knew then our interior design was working."

—BARBARA DIETZEL

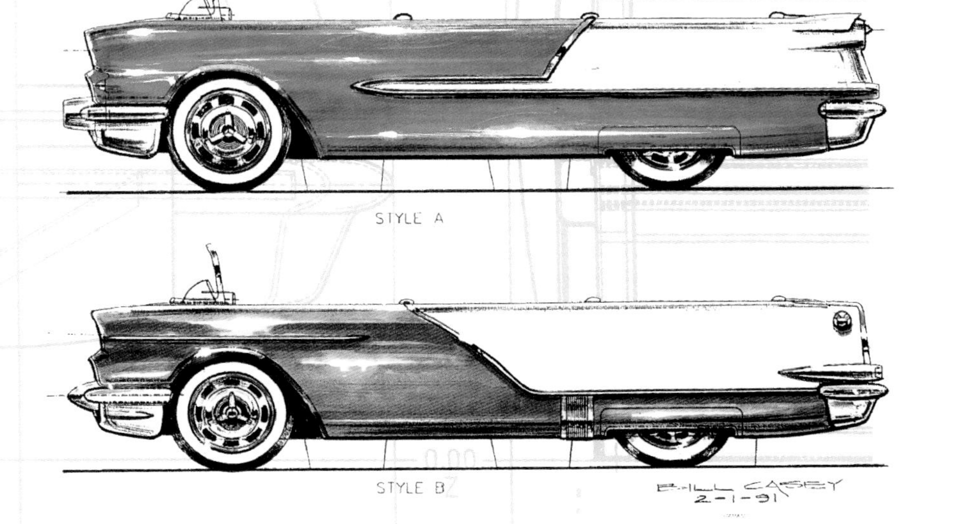

"Walt looked at every single graphic that went into the park, not just the main marquees. He knew them all. Along with everything else that established a sense of what the park was all about, they were well thought out. I still look at them and learn from them today."

—RUDY LORD

VISUAL COMMUNICATIONS: GRAPHICS

Four thousand, four hundred and fifty-five signs, including ride and show marquees, operational signs, show graphics, posters and menus were designed and produced for Disneyland Paris. Given that, you can imagine how many graphic designs have been developed at Imagineering over the years for our projects. From simple directional signs to elegant attraction posters, and everything in between, Imagineers have designed and produced just about every graphic you have ever seen in a Disney theme park.

Signs are an integral part of the stories we tell in our parks. Along with effectively communicating a message in words, our graphic designs must reflect and complement the overall style and story of a ride, show or attraction.

The graphics for a project evolve right along with the development of an idea. As soon as show writers create preliminary nomenclature, the graphic designers get busy putting pencil to paper (or stylus to computer). While designing, a great deal of research is done, both for inspiration and to accurately capture the graphic essence of a project's theme.

"While art-directing the installation of the graphics to make sure the finished signage matches all specifications, you can usually adjust things like light levels, color tone and positioning. But when we installed the 9-ton marquee at The Land pavilion in Epcot, it was a case of 'you'd better do it right the first time!'"

—LETICIA LELEVIER

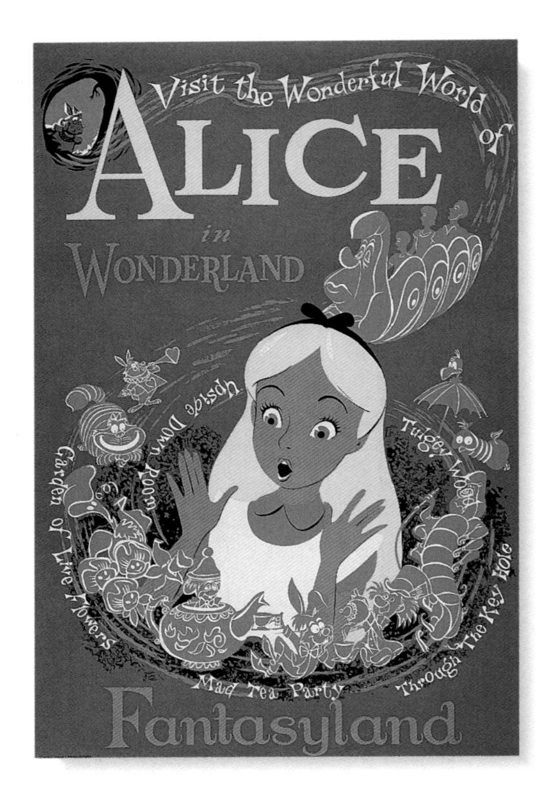
Visit the Wonderful World of
ALICE
in
WONDERLAND
Upside Down Room
Tulgey Wood
Garden of Live Flowers
Mad Tea Party
Through The Key Hole
Fantasyland

GATEWAY to ENCHANTMENT
Storybook Land
Fantasyland

CLIMB THE STAIRWAY TO HIGH ADVENTURE!
SWISS FAMILY
TREEHOUSE
ADVENTURELAND

NATURE'S WONDERLAND
VIA THE MINE TRAIN THRU RAINBOW CAVERNS
OLYMPIC ELK
BEAVER VALLEY
BEAR COUNTRY
LIVING DESERT
FRONTIERLAND

FLY YOUR OWN
FLYING SAUCER
space terminal in
TOMORROWLAND

ADVENTURE
THRU
INNER
SPACE
Presented by
Monsanto
TOMORROWLAND

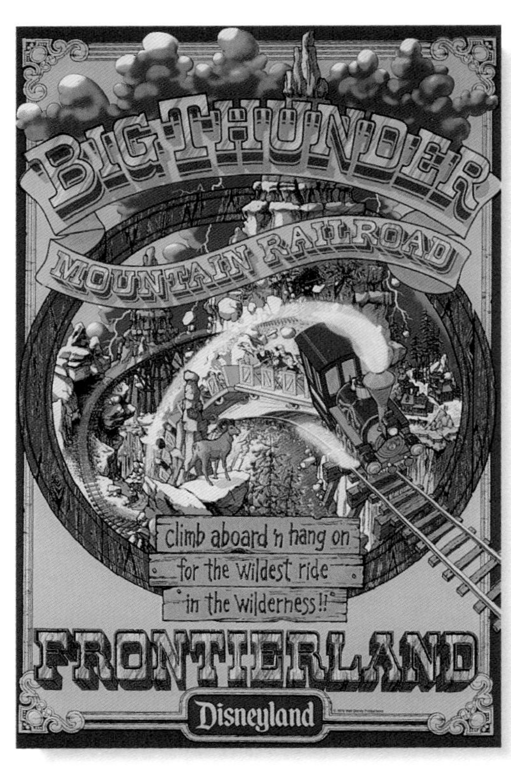
BIG THUNDER
MOUNTAIN RAILROAD
climb aboard 'n hang on
for the wildest ride
in the wilderness!!
FRONTIERLAND
Disneyland

THE HALL OF
PRESIDENTS
LIBERTY SQUARE
The Great Moments
The Great Men

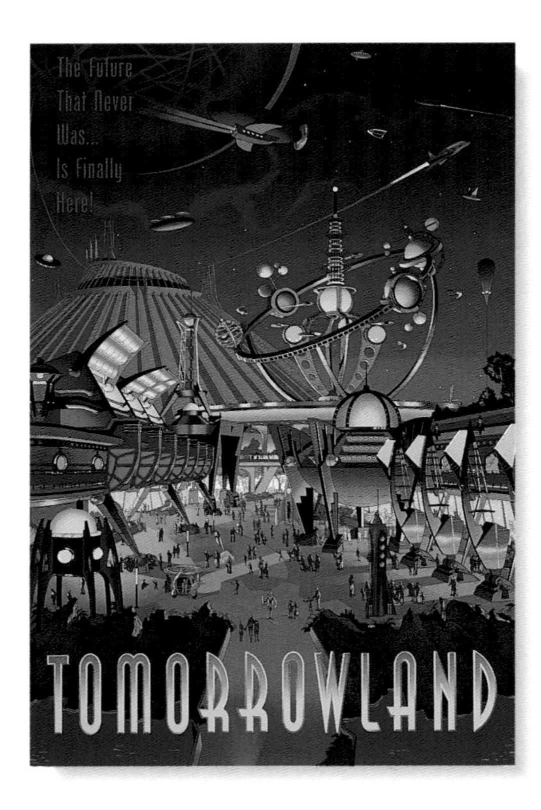
The Future
That Never
Was...
Is Finally
Here!
TOMORROWLAND

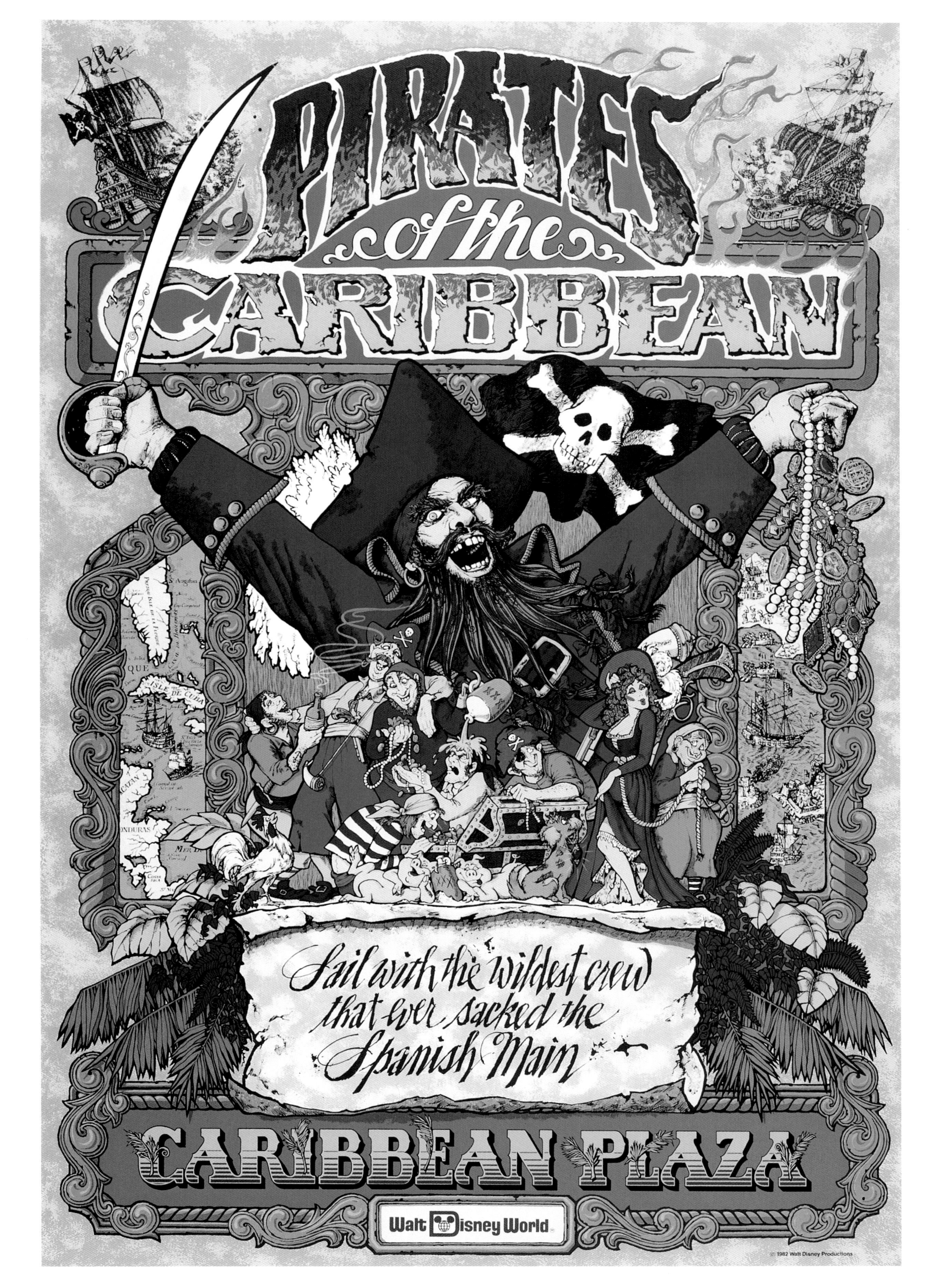

PIRATES
of the
CARIBBEAN
ISLE DE CUBA
Sail with the wildest crew
that ever sacked the
Spanish Main
CARIBBEAN PLAZA
Walt Disney World
© 1982 Walt Disney Productions

See the giant squid from...
20,000 Leagues
UNDER THE Sea
TOMORROWLAND

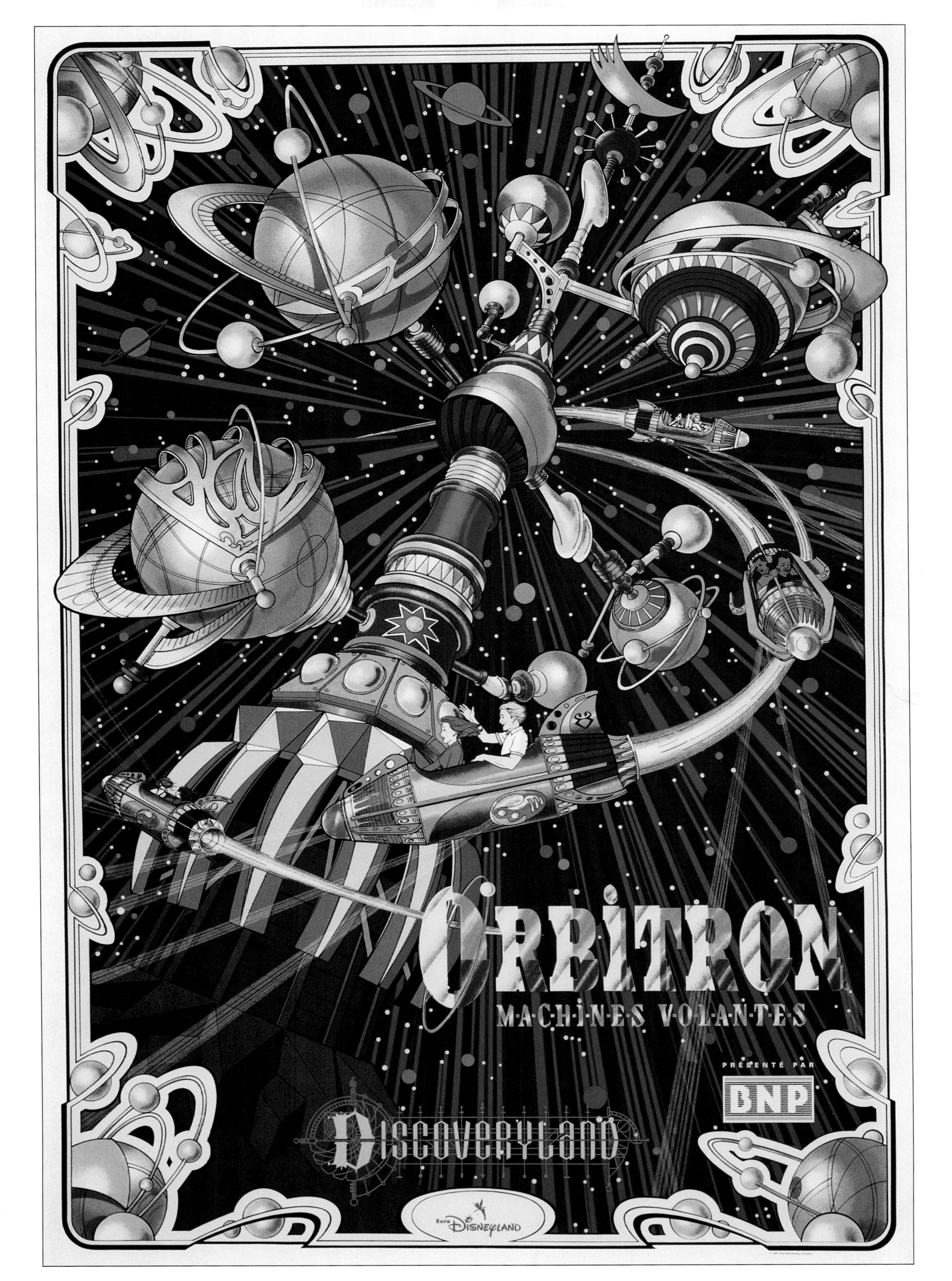
ORBİTRON
MACHİNES VOLANTES
PRÉSENTÉ PAR
BNP
DISCOVERYLAND
Euro DISNEYLAND

Can you conquer the evil forces of the Disney Villains?
あなたはディズニーの悪役たちに勝てるかな？
CINDERELLA CASTLE
MYSTERY TOUR
シンデレラ城 ミステリーツアー
FANTASYLAND
ファンタジーランド
Tokyo
Disneyland
© 1986 The Walt Disney Company

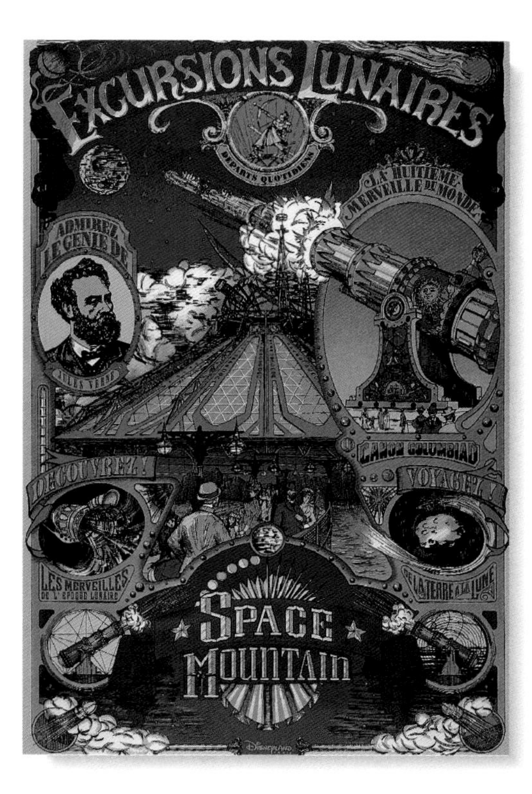

PAGES 102–107: Disney Attraction Posters represent a unique blending of illustration and graphic design through various fine art printing techniques. These vivid images were originally created to introduce park guests to the wide diversity of attractions available for their enjoyment during current and future visits to Disneyland. Today, there are over one hundred and twenty attraction posters heralding the adventure, fantasy, and wonder to be found at Disney parks around the world. The collec-tion presented here represents the four-decade-long evolution of this unique art form. Early posters, such as Nature's Wonderland and 20,000 Leagues Under the Sea, were created entirely by hand using stencils mounted on silk fabric. The limited colors and highly stylized design elements stimulate the viewer's imagination. Recent posters, such as Cinderella Castle Mystery Tour and Grand Canyon, utilize state-of-the-art screen printing technologies to create complex and dramatic images possible only through this technique. Interpretation from the original concept to the finished poster requires as many as forty separate print runs to achieve the wide range of color typical in these posters.

LEFT: In this early concept sketch, vehicle designer George McGinnis set out to prove that Imagineering's experimental twelve-passenger "motion-base" vehicle could be transformed into the kind of troop transport that even a famous archeologist like Indiana Jones would dig.

BELOW: Once the ride vehicle was designed, artist Chuck Ballew put the concept in gear by showing what it would look like filled with passengers, speeding out of control through the ancient corridors of the Lost Temple.

More than just a ride

The rides and attractions we dream up are often sophisticated beyond existing technology, since they must be durable enough to operate every few minutes, every day, 365 days a year, and exceed the standards of all local building codes. In addition, they must achieve and maintain the highest safety standard in the industry.

To provide a visually exciting ride vehicle body to wrap around all this technology, we have designers who conceptualize the vehicle in sketch form, detailed paintings, and on computer. Once a vehicle body design exists in the computer, its every line and angle can be studied, adjusted and refined. This computer-generated vehicle model can even be placed on an electronic rendition of the proposed ride track, and animated to simulate how the entire system would work when completed. We can accomplish this computer animation from a plan-view, looking straight down over the entire ride system, or from the point of view of a passenger actually experiencing the ride.

Full-sized drawings of vehicles are generated from the computer model to study size relationships to passengers. Scale models are made to bring the design into a physical dimension. Finally, a full-sized clay model is rendered, the last step before the actual bodies are fabricated and attached.

"Any ride engineer can design parts. But it is a unique kind of engineer who can blend a creative story and theme with practical technology. To continue to rise to the standard-setting challenge as a ride engineer here, you have to be more than a nuts and bolts type of person. You have to be a big thinker, a 'blank sheet of paper' person."

—DON HILSEN

TOP LEFT: While a young industrial design student at Art Center School of Design in Pasadena in 1966, George McGinnis was taken by surprise when Walt Disney dropped by one day and asked if he would be interested in designing vehicles for rides. Since that time, George has been involved in a wide variety of vehicle designs, from Mark V and VI Monorails to the troop transports for the Indiana Jones Adventure at Disneyland.

BELOW: A prototype troop transport vehicle undergoes preliminary motion programming and testing inside the Imagineering vehicle test facility at Valencia, California. All of the "dips" and "bumps" you feel while riding in the Indiana Jones Adventure were computer-programmed to happen at the appropriate moments within the ride. This motion program was created in "real time" by a ride engineer who rode in the back seat while the vehicle negotiated the track—over and over again!

OVERLEAF: Long before the Indiana Jones Adventure was built, artist Bryan Jowers created this powerful scene to get everyone excited about the thrilling potential for the project.

"A week and a half after Disneyland opened, only one Autopia car was still working. We had to invent and re-invent a way to keep all the darn things working all the time."

—BOB GURR

LEFT: This 1958 painting of the sailing ship *Columbia* was created by Sam McKim to show how the first U.S. vessel ever to circumnavigate the globe might appear on the Rivers of America at Disneyland.

BELOW: The design of the traditional Main Street horse-drawn trolley was modified to show how it would appear as an enclosed, weather-protected vehicle at Disneyland Paris, as seen in this drawing by Tom Yorke.

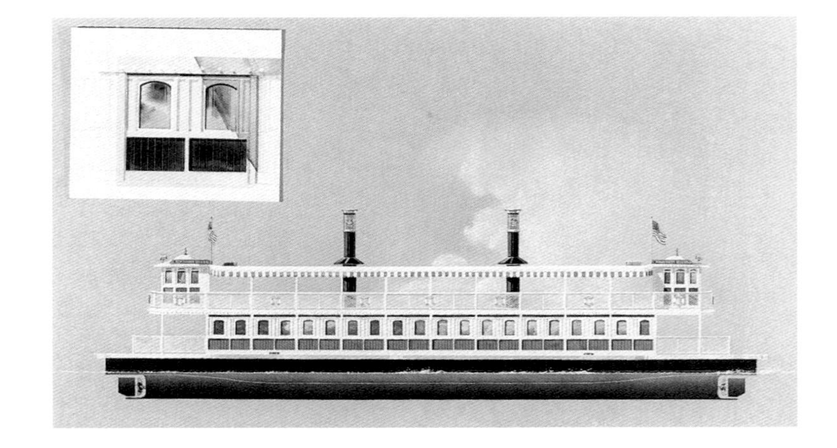

ABOVE: Vehicles designed for Disney theme parks must help to tell our story as well as be functional. In this pencil sketch, Bob Gurr designed an "omnibus" that could transport guests up and down Main Street at Disneyland while being part of the scene.

RIGHT ABOVE: Harper Goff launched the first riverboat design for the Jungle Cruise with this sketch.

RIGHT BELOW: Even though the monorail could accommodate large numbers of guests who needed transportation between the Ticket and Transportation Center and the main entrance to the Magic Kingdom located across the Seven Seas Lagoon, the success that came with the first year of the Walt Disney World Resort meant that additional capacity was required. The need to create another means of transportation brought about the launching of the ferry boats in 1972. The Staten Island Ferry served as the inspiration for this design of the "Kingdom Queen."

"The statistics are very much against us. Think about it. If there is a one in a million chance something will go wrong, and ten million guests ride our ride, then something will happen ten times. We can't design to that one in a million. We have to design to one in hundreds of millions."

—BRUCE JOHNSON

ABOVE: The Jolly Trolley heads for downtown Toontown in this concept sketch by Marcelo Vignali.

ABOVE: While Epcot was in its concept design stage, special consideration was given to the ride vehicle designs for the attractions in Future World. To be part of the theme, they had to present a "future industrial" simple, but streamlined appearance. This was Gil Keppler's initial concept for the Spaceship Earth OmniMover.

NEAR RIGHT: This design for the original Autopia was developed by Bob Gurr in 1954—the same year the first Corvette hit the streets.

FAR RIGHT: This turn of the century science fiction design of the Orbitron Rocket for Discoveryland at Disneyland Paris fits in nicely with the "Jules Verne" styling influence of the land, as seen in this rendering by Andy Probert.

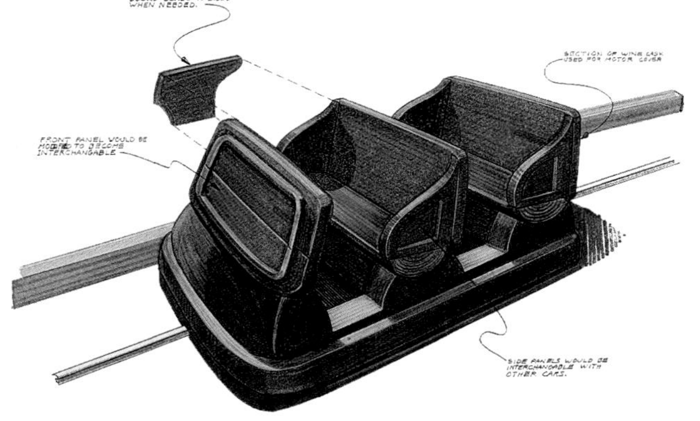

LEFT: Bill Bohn designed this "wooden" ride vehicle for Pinocchio's Daring Journey introduced at Tokyo Disneyland in 1983. The vehicle was designed to accommodate removable front panels so that individual sections fabricated with a character, such as Jiminy Cricket, could be easily added or replaced.

BELOW: To increase ride capacity, this vehicle for Space Mountain at Disneyland Paris was designed with a side-by-side, as opposed to an "in-line" seating configuration. Note the Discoveryland-style side panels seen in this sketch by Mark Stutz.

Dreams do not come true all by themselves. They are nourished by the bounty that comes of hard work.

ABOVE: Sam McKim created this sketch of the "Fred Gurley," the third train added to the Disneyland Railroad, which featured the new open-air "Excursion Cars" inspired by actual railroad cars that were used during the summer months for rides in the country.

LEFT: Bob McDonald's steam train was right on track with Howard Cronanworth's graphic design to communicate the rustic theme of the Fort Wilderness Campground at Walt Disney World. This poster is proof that an arrangement of carefully selected letters can tell a story in more ways than one.

BELOW: Just as colorboards are created to indicate the color palette for buildings and interiors, they can also be used for an attraction, as is the case with this board by Tom Yorke, created for the Disneyland Paris Railroad. "All aboard!"

TRAIN OF THOUGHT

Walt Disney was always fascinated with technology. His life-long interest in all things mechanical probably began with his boyhood love for trains. Experiences that centered around them and on them were among the fondest memories of his youth. As the story goes, Mickey Mouse himself was born on a train.

Sometimes seeking relaxation after a busy day at the Studio, Walt would stop by the nearby Glendale station to walk alongside the tracks and watch the trains come and go. He eventually built his own railroad, the Carolwood Pacific, which included a small-scale train he could actually ride aboard as it traveled around his Holmby Hills backyard in west Los Angeles.

When he first began to seriously consider his theme park idea, Walt wrote himself a memo outlining his thoughts and dreams. On top of the list was the description of a railroad station that would be situated prominently at the entrance to the park.

Walt loved the experiences of his past, but he was also a futurist. Walt's most optimistic dream was to introduce people to the benefits of future technologies—not only in the theme parks, but in the real world. Just as he re-invented the amusement park with the opening of Disneyland, he wanted to take his success a giant leap further by attempting to solve the problems of many cities, particularly the lack of effective transportation systems.

In 1959 Walt introduced at Disneyland the first operating monorail system in the Western

ABOVE LEFT: In his 1953 series of Fantasyland drawings, Bruce Bushman sketched what he had envisioned Casey Jr. might be for Disneyland.

LEFT: Just outside the original roundhouse at Disneyland, the E.P. Ripley receives some last minute touchups before being fired up for its first of many excursions around the park. Since this photo was taken in 1955, the trains at Disneyland have traveled a distance that equals circling the globe more than 150 times.

ABOVE: After Casey Jr. came down the track at Disneyland, it was the only one in existence for over 40 years. When the little circus train finally said "I think I can exist in another Disney theme park," Jim Shull conceptualized how it might climb the hill into Disneyland Paris.

FAR LEFT, BELOW: Engineer Walt proudly high-balling the fourth addition to the Disneyland Railroad—the "Ernest S. Marsh"—from the Main Street Station.

NEAR LEFT, BELOW: Honorary Carolwood Pacific Railroad engineer Ward Kimball takes passenger Salvador Dali on a sur-rail trip around Walt Disney's Holmby Hills backyard. The Carolwood Pacific's engine "Lilly Belle"—now on display in the Main Street Station at Disneyland—was the original inspiration and model for the Disneyland Railroad. Who would have guessed that nostalgic little backyard engine would have been powerful enough to pull the past right into the future?

BOTTOM: Bruce Bushman created this design for Casey Jr. at Disneyland.

Hemisphere as a demonstration to civic leaders that the future was on their doorstep. The success of the WED-designed and built monorail proved to the Imagineers they were capable of opening the door to the future, not only in efficient transportation systems, but in all things technical.

Thanks to Walt's love for trains and the Disneyland Railroad, many subsequent transportation innovations and offshoot technologies have been introduced in Disney theme parks and to the world. These range from Omnimovers that carry 2,500 guests per hour through an attraction, to Imagineering Labs' DisneyVision magic carpet flight through "the whole new (virtual) world" of *Aladdin*.

ABOVE: Herbert Ryman's proposal for the entrance to the original Tomorrowland was framed by Walt's vision of the transportation system of the future.

INSET ABOVE: This suspended monorail was loosely inspired by a magazine photo of the French "Safege" system which was not actually built until 1958. An experimental model, the Safege only traveled under one mile of test track.

BELOW LEFT: Walt Disney with Richard Nixon and his family dedicating the monorail at Disneyland in 1959. A consulting Alweg engineer could not believe his eyes when the Imagineers had their monorail up and running in such a short time. Bob Gurr, a vehicle designer for Imagineering at the time, recalled when then-vice president Richard Nixon officially launched the first train. "That Alweg engineer was astounded," remembered Bob. "He said, 'we never put the public on a train in less than seven years. In six months' time, you Americans put your own vice president on one!'" Bob continued, "It was then I realized what we did at WED."

BELOW: John Hench added polish to Bob Gurr's black and white pencil design of the Disneyland-Alweg Monorail by giving the trains color and highlights.

LEFT: George McGinnis, styling designer of the Mark IV Monorails at Walt Disney World, showed how this "transportation of the future" would provide convenient "drive-through service" for guests staying at the Contemporary Resort Hotel.

BELOW: At the Walt Disney World Resort, these Imagineering-designed Mark VI Monorails safely and efficiently carry more than 110,000 passengers a day with a reliability rate of 99.9%. From 1971 to today, they have traveled over four million miles.

"Technologically speaking, Walt was always looking to the future. When we began working on the animated pirates, our ideas and innovations, amazing as they were, couldn't come soon enough. He'd say, 'that's fine for Mach 1. But I'm thinking Mach 3.'"

—SAM McKIM

ANIMATING IN THREE DIMENSIONS

In 1949, while visiting New Orleans, Walt purchased a tiny mechanical bird. Intrigued by its lifelike movements, Walt envisioned the possibility of creating animated movement in three dimensions. He gave the bird to Roger Broggie, head of the Studio machine shop, and asked him to discover how it worked.

Walt's long-term plan was to develop this new form of dimensional animation for use in the new park. As a start, he asked animation art director Ken Anderson to help him develop a miniature "dancing man." Ken's acceptance of this challenge made him the first Imagineer.

The nine-inch-high dancing man was prompted into movement by metal cams located directly beneath the figure. After filming Buddy Ebsen performing a dance routine, the movements of the figure were adjusted to replicate Buddy's movements.

The next experiment was a miniature barbershop quartet—the first attempt at synchronized mouth movement, as the four "sang" along to pre-recorded music. Like the dancing man, the quartet—and the hidden mechanisms that moved them—was situated in a 3′ x 3′ support cabinet. The main mechanism located within the lower portion of the cabinet was a large spinning drum. As the drum rotated, the edge of a cam traveling along its surface registered levers that pulled wires connected to the characters' feet to make them move—a reverse marionette.

The tremendous push to open Disneyland put a damper on the strides WED was making with the animated figures. The plan for opening day did, however, include two animated figures, crude as they were. Motion picture special effects man Bob Mattey, Sr. helped to develop the Indian Chief who, while sitting on a horse, waved at the boats traveling by on the Rivers of America, and a dancing native found along the shores of the Jungle Cruise. These "cam and lever" figures, however, were only capable of simple, repetitive motions.

Soon after the park was opened, Walt decided to create a talking "Confucius" head that would greet guests as they approached a proposed Chinese restaurant for Disneyland. Although its prototype rubber face mask deteriorated rapidly during testing, the mechanics in the head proved successful.

Around that same time, artist John Hench showed Walt a concept rendering that presented an idea for a tropical-themed restaurant. The painting featured several colorful birds that were located on perches directly above the tables. "I'm not too sure about this idea, John," said Walt as he studied the painting. "The birds will be pooping on the tables." John laughed, and responded, "These aren't real birds, Walt. These are all animated!"

The restaurant idea was dropped, but the animated birds were created to perform in the first fully-orchestrated Audio-Animatronics show ever—Walt Disney's Enchanted Tiki Room.

Walt was so pleased with the birds and the progress being made on the Chinese Head, he decided one head would not be good enough. So work began on the Hall of Presidents, part of a proposed area behind Main Street called Liberty Street. Originally intended for that show, the first prototype Audio-Animatronics human figure made was Abraham Lincoln. In the early stages of its development, some of the Imagineers thought that, since the figure was not moving as realistically as they had hoped, perhaps they should make Mr. Lincoln more of a stylized, cartoon-like figure. "No." Walt told them. "I want him to breathe. I want him to be alive!"

The robin that sang along with Mary Poppins, in the 1964 motion picture of the same name, was developed by WED. Thanks to the success of the film, its profits were used to construct the building that housed the staff and equipment necessary to design and build Audio-Animatronics performers, animated props, and elaborate show sets. Starting with

OPPOSITE: **Perhaps the very first work of Imagineering art (from a collection of more than 50,000 pieces), this 1949 rendering by Ken Anderson was done at Walt's request to design a stage for the miniature "Dancing Man." This piece had been misplaced for more than forty years, until, in doing research for this book, it was discovered by Randy Webster in the "Golden Horseshoe" file in the Imagineering Art Library.**

LEFT: **The actual miniature stage inspired by Ken Anderson's rendering was built—for the most part—by Walt Disney himself. Walt and Ken drove all over town searching several hobby shops and hardware stores to find just the right wooden ornaments and moldings for the project. Walt even tried to carve the little figure himself. But eventually, he decided he had better get a sculptor to do it and enlisted the skills of Cristodoro. Note the Bell and Howell movie projector on the floor of the display. The projector served a dual purpose: As its motor turned the hand-cut cams to move the figure, its synchronized film provided the sound track.**

ABOVE: **In 1963, in a conference room located in the original WED facility on Sonora Street in Glendale, Walt Disney acted out how he wanted Mr. Lincoln to perform at the fair.**

fifteen people headed by Roger Broggie, this animation research and development group became an official WED division named MAPO after *Mary Poppins*.

The original MAPO building, located directly behind Imagineering headquarters in Glendale, California, was converted to a model shop and show design space after MAPO outgrew the facility and moved to larger accommodations in North Hollywood, a few miles north. Along with their move came a new meaning for their name, which became an acronym for Manufacturing And Production Organization. MAPO has built every three-dimensional animated figure and prop that has ever come to life in a dimensional Disney show.

The design of a dimensional character, human or otherwise, begins on paper in concept sketch form. Several variations of a proposed character are sketched before a final choice is made. Once a character design is approved by Imagineering leaders, a sculptor will meet with the figure production team—those who will actually build the final character—to discuss the figure's intended role in the story, movements, and special requirements. The sculptor will draw more detailed sketches to use specifically as a model for transforming the design into a three-dimensional study maquette. The maquette becomes the model from which the character will be sculpted to size.

Imagineering sculptors are unique to the medium. As they sculpt, they must do so with a keen understanding of the idiosyncrasies and limitations of an Audio-Animatronics figure—its "motion profile." They must think ahead, being sensitive while they work to the intended movements of the character that is now lifeless clay.

The first Imagineer to realize he must sculpt in a manner that would allow his work to eventually "come to life" was Blaine Gibson. "The things we sculpted may have been animated mechanically, but if they already had a spark of life inherent in their conceptualization, then they worked even better," said Blaine. "There has to be something that gets the viewer involved, and the sculptor has to be involved even before that."

When most sculptors complete their work, it is considered a finished work of art. When an Imagineering sculptor completes his work, the piece serves as a "next step" in developing the final theme park character. From this full-sized clay sculpture, a detail-exact plaster cast will be made. From this cast, the final character will begin to evolve.

A special blend of molten rubber is poured into the cast, and once cured, becomes the character's pliable exterior skin. This skin-like rubber can be made in any color, depending upon whether it is going to be a green space alien, a human or a singing banana. Meanwhile, an aluminum structural frame is fabricated to serve as the character's "skeleton." All of the intricate inner workings and mechanics of the character are attached to the jointed frame. A hard clear plastic material is then created in the shape of the character, to both shield and contain its mechanical insides, and to serve as a solid foundation upon which the soft rubber skin is finally attached.

Once this inner and outer structure of the character is completed, including the eyes, teeth and contoured skin, it is brought to the "fur and feather" (figure finishing) department for make-up, wigs, eyelashes, eyebrows, and additional accessories such as hats or eyeglasses. Finally, specially-designed clothing is custom tailored to provide the character with a costume appropriate to its role in the show.

Whatever their shape, size or function, all of our three-dimensional animated figures are created for one purpose—to bring our story *to life*.

AUDIO-ANIMATRONICS: ACTING THE PART

ABOVE: This show-programming tool called an Animation Console (Anacon) brings Audio-Animatronics figures, show lights and animated props to life. Each knob and button corresponds with an individual motion, such as an eye blink or head nod. As the show programmer animates a figure in sequence with the audio track, each movement is collectively stored. The entire show sequence is then transferred to a Digital Animation Control System (DACS) for automated playback.

ABOVE RIGHT: In the early days of show programming, figures and other show equipment would sometimes break down. Whenever film animator-turned-show programmer Bill Justice waited for system repairs, he would add a little character to the Anacon.

Animated characters seen on film are photographed one drawing, or one film frame, at a time. When the film is projected at twenty-four frames per second, the characters come to life. Audio-Animatronics figures are brought to life one frame at a time as well. In this case, the frames are actually electronic signals. Each figure movement is programmed by an Imagineering animator using an animation control console ("Anacon") one electronic frame at a time, and this information is digitally recorded on computer disks. The completed program is then transferred to a sophisticated computerized signal controller located "backstage." This controller sends the programmed digital signals—twenty four electronic frames per second—out to the various mechanisms that cause the figure to move.

In the early days of figure programming, such as for the Mr. Lincoln figure, the frames of movement were recorded on reel-to-reel magnetic audio tapes. When played back, the tapes generated audio signals that triggered the mechanisms that caused the figure to move—synchronized with recorded dialogue, music and special effects. Even though digital disks have replaced audio tapes, we pay homage to Walt's original idea by still calling this form of three-dimensional animation Audio-Animatronics.

RIGHT: From left to right, pioneers Jack Taylor, Bill Justice, Marc Davis and Wathel Rogers work on two of the dozens of "cam cabinets" used to create the character action in Pirates of the Caribbean. Each of the cams that turned inside the cabinets was responsible for generating a certain figure movement. Turning all together, the physical motion cams brought the "actors" to life. The cam system has long since been replaced by DACS which sends motion commands electronically.

"We ran the wiring for the Mary Poppins robin through its feet. The first one we made wasn't quite insulated enough and there was a slight electrical current running from it right through Julie Andrews' finger. She was astonished. I can still see her trying like crazy to shake it off."

—ROGER BROGGIE, JR.

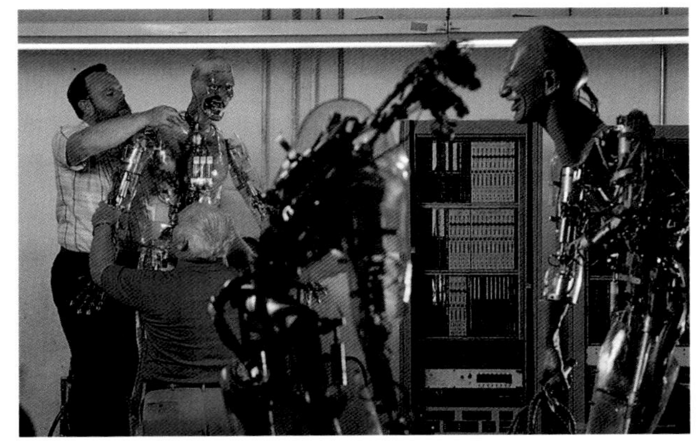

"There is nothing technical out there in the world that can put up with the kinds of abuse our Audio-Animatronics figures put up with in our parks. When we design our figures, our criteria is far more stringent than the criteria established even for aircraft."

—BRUCE JOHNSON

ABOVE: MAPO Animation experts Larry Sheldon and Stan Abrahamson prepare Epcot figures for a trial run. Note the DACS cabinets in the background.

RIGHT: SIR—the Simulated Intelligence Robot—demonstrates the latest in teleportation technology at Alien Encounter in Tomorrowland at the Magic Kingdom.

BELOW: Small shows or scenes of shows are usually programmed, tested, and approved at our North Hollywood facility. After a figure is installed in the "field," a show programmer arrives to fine-tune its movements so it can interact effectively with all of the other show elements. Michael Sprout is pictured here at Tokyo Disneyland orchestrating all of the animated elements of the pizza-making machine from outer space for the Pan Galactic Pizza Show.

LEFT: **Bob Joslin fires up a hot new special effect for testing inside the Illusioneering Lab before it is approved and installed in the field.**

BELOW: **A magical troll dust special effect passes the "ooh" and "aah" test before being shipped to the Maelstrom attraction in the Norway Pavilion at Epcot.**

LEFT: **These Illusioneers erupt with excitement while demonstrating how their "boiling" lava is really pretty cool. Yale Gracey (left) is considered the "father" of Illusioneering.**

"It wouldn't be a special effect if it worked the first time we installed it."

—RAY JONES

SPECIAL EFFECTS: ILLUSIONEERING

Special effects in motion pictures always look spectacular because the best take—whether physically choreographed or computer generated—has been selected and edited, and captured forever on film. In our theme parks, there is no such thing as a second take. The effects must always look spectacular in one take, every few minutes, every single day. We call this the art of Illusioneering.

Because we must conform to strict building codes and consider the close proximity of our guests to our special effects, their design and execution must be safe as well as visually and physically exciting. Illusioneers are masters at creating fire that does not really burn, explosions that do not actually destroy, bubbling, molten lava that is cool to the touch (and safe even if eaten) and dense fog that is safe to breathe. The materials of choice are those that are dry, non-toxic and leave no residue. Where an oil-based smoke effect can be used on a temporary movie set without a lot of worry, we must create a different type of smoke that does not leave a coat of oil behind on animated figures and their costumes, ride vehicles, theater seats and guests. If a blast of steam is required for a movie shot, a small source tank will suffice. But when several cannons and pistols must constantly fire in Pirates of the Caribbean, they require a massive permanent boiler and an elaborate system of piping to keep the steam coming strong. And because our ride and show effects are continuous, each and every one must be frequently checked and regularly maintained.

Most of the equipment used to create all of our effects is not purchased, or readily available, but is designed, tested and manufactured at Imagineering. There is always something bubbling, exploding, floating, popping, glowing or dripping in our effects lab. The moment an Illusioneer finds out the effects requirements for a show, he or she gets to work defying the odds, logic and the laws of nature.

An imagineered special effect can be as tiny as a flittering firefly or as grand as seven-story-high fiery explosion. It may be continuous like water gently rippling in the moonlight on a flat scenic painting, or precisely timed to occur at just the right moment in a show, like the thousands of escaping mice running underfoot in the Honey, I Shrunk the Audience theater. Most of our special effects are programmed to work in perfect concert with other supporting show elements, such as controlled lighting, animated figures, animated props, musical score and ride vehicle location.

As amazing or convincing as the effect may be, it is never considered a show in itself, but as one part of the whole story. An imagineered special effect is an illusion, but because it occurs in front of you in real time, in a real place, it helps make our story real.

"I relate what we do to ballet. The dancer makes it look easy although it is difficult to do. Their legs have to be so strong, and yet, they are so graceful."

—DAVE TAYLOR

ABOVE: A powerful Tesla coil being developed for the Maelstrom attraction in the Norway pavilion at World Showcase shoots giant bolts of electricity within a few feet of these very brave Imagineering volunteers.

BELOW: A port o'call just off the Spanish Main is engulfed in flames as the Pirates of the Caribbean go on a rampage in Adventureland at Disneyland Paris. When the original Pirates of the Caribbean was under construction at Disneyland in 1967, the fire marshal asked the Imagineering special effects designers to install a system that would turn off the fire effect in the event of a real fire, so the fire department wouldn't spend its time in a futile fight against artificial flames. Twenty-five years later, when the Disneyland Paris fire effect was first turned on, the French fire marshals thought the flames were real—and Adventureland designer Chris Tietz had to stop them from calling in a real fire alarm!

RIGHT: Yale Gracey (right) proves that he has a grasp on the spooky special effects for the Haunted Mansion at Disneyland.

"If Imagineering begins with a spark, R&D is about triggering a meteor shower!"

—MARSHALL MONROE

IMAGINEERING LABS

ABOVE: Illumination experts test a giant servo controlled spotlight.

Imagineering's commitment to curiosity and exploration takes a particularly mercurial form in our Research and Development Division. Cloaked in an aura of mystery and secrecy, these techno-wizards discover, invent and present the state-of-the-art technologies that will enchant our future attractions.

This inquisitive team includes inventors, scientists (mad, rocket and otherwise), chemists, programmers, camera and lens designers, materials specialists, mechanical gadgeteers, machinists, ecologists, circuit designers, illusionists and even roller coaster and G-force experts. Together they explore new possibilities for the shows, events, interactions and accommodations that constitute the Disney "guest experience." With just over 100 talented thinkers, they are the largest research group in the world focusing exclusively on storytelling technology.

They're literally "all over the map."

R & D is spread throughout three primary facilities located in Glendale, California, East Hampton, New York, and Orlando, Florida, each containing everything you would expect to find in Merlin's workshop. Gadgets whiz, gizmos whir, exotic colorful potions bubble away. Using research, theory, simulation software and good ol' fashioned empiricism, the team works with other key divisions of Imagineering to develop everything from next-generation rides and Audio-Animatronics figures to controls and cyberspace destinations.

"R&D's mission is simple: we are inventing the future of the company."

—BRAN FERREN

Inspiration for investigation can come from any number of in-house sources. Sometimes the intuition of one of our inventors or mad scientists results in a mock-up that in turn inspires a show designer. Other R & D projects evolve from collaborations with show designers who are looking ahead to their next project. In this case, the designer relates a new type of story or impression he or she is considering. The R & D team creates the experience (almost always a novel working prototype that illustrates the concept), giving everyone involved the chance to evaluate its viability. This is a pivotal step, since R & D's mission includes exploring technology from the human side—not only how and why things function, but whether or not they are effective *emotionally*. If the show designer sees potential, the production department takes over to make the idea real. In all cases, prototypes are in "sketch" form, allowing for rapid modification and iteration.

It is no accident that Imagineering holds 28 patents and in 1996 had more than 50 others pending in such areas as special effects, ride systems, projection systems, interactive technology, live entertainment, fiber optics and advanced audio systems.

R & D has initiated technologies as wide-ranging as the four-wheel steering motion base found in the Indiana Jones ride, to the wave machine at Typhoon Lagoon Water Adventure Park at Walt Disney World, to the software and hardware foundations of the fledgling VR studio.

"Avoiding subtlety" is an important part of this equation. R & D is about pushing the envelope both technically and creatively. For this reason, a typical day at R & D might consist of inventing the world's first interactive simulator-based ride system, the world's best computer graphic characters or some other ground-breaking one-of-a-kind gizmo designed to make our guests' experience more enjoyable.

Despite the apparent emphasis on technology, one philosophy remains constant through all R & D projects—the technology serves creativity. This is what we like to call "technology for the right reason." The Walt Disney Company is in the business of telling stories. This drives everything our R & D department does. We strive to attract and retain the world's top talent for mixing the arts, sciences, engineering and design. That includes a resident concept team whose job is to keep the R & D techies abreast of where society, our guests, and the culture are going. This information is reflected in both the technology and the creative uses of that technology throughout our parks and related venues.

One of the lesser known yet vitally important charters of our R & D team is to develop "environmentally friendly" ways of doing and creating new things—from materials, such as fabrics and plastics, to natural habitat management. Often the benefits of the research done by our environmental engineers extends beyond the berm of our parks. For instance, R & D implemented a revolutionary method of controlling pests by introducing their natural enemies to protect the barrier hedges at Disneyland. This solution has been very successful, contributing to the reduction of pesticide use throughout southern California. R & D work at The Living Seas pavilion at Epcot functions as good show while advancing knowledge bases that benefit society. Scientists work on a variety of projects there, one of which is their invention of the "Dolphin Keyboard." This keyboard is used to help better understand the cognitive behavior of dolphins, allowing them to communicate with divers by pressing certain keys on the board that represent words.

The focus of Imagineering Research and Development is, of course, entertainment. But while working on their many technical and environmental wonders and amazing off-shoot discoveries for Imagineering, they are working on ways to change the world.

Dreams tend to ignore conventional means.

ABOVE: Living Seas Researchers converse with dolphins using the patented underwater keyboard developed and constructed by Research and Development.

ABOVE RIGHT: Scientist Kathleen Nelson experiments with advanced skin polymers for Audio-Animatronics figures.

TOP: Researchers use advanced equipment like this custom digital scanning electron microscope.

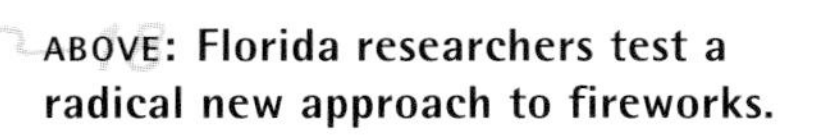

ABOVE: Florida researchers test a radical new approach to fireworks.

ABOVE: Optics and Image Processing research involves test bench flexibility coupled with laser precision.

LEFT: Guests playtest a Virtual Reality prototype as part of Research and Development's computer graphics research.

"When guests notice the waterways at Walt Disney World and think they're beautiful, they don't realize their beauty is the result of a highly engineered system."

—BEN SCHWEGLER

Theme Park Productions

When Walt Disney made *Fantasia*, he wanted the film to travel through the projector horizontally to attain a wider image. Theater owners, however, refused to retrofit their equipment to accommodate such a radical change. Disneyland allowed Walt the freedom to experiment with new ways to use film and provided him with the opportunity to become his own exhibitor, to invent not only exotic new cameras and unique film formats, but the specialized theaters in which to present them. He began to integrate films into shows like Circle-Vision and Flight to the Moon, and he began to turn theaters into attractions.

Today more than three hundred films—presented in thirteen different formats—entertain guests in our parks. These formats are Circle-Vision, single-panel (screen) 16mm, single-panel 35mm, single-panel 70mm, three-panel 70mm, five-panel 35mm, five-panel 70mm, Omni-Max 70mm, 3D 70mm, video projection, interactive, "Pepper's Ghost" reflective screen, and projection through fiber optic bands.

Because film and video play such an important role in a majority of our rides, shows and attractions, a new division of Imagineering, called "Theme Park Productions," was formed to create and produce them. This division is responsible for everything from video presentations within attractions, like the ExtraTERRORestrial Alien Encounter, to major attractions themselves, like Honey, I Shrunk the Audience.

Most entertainment companies simply make do by renting Panavision equipment. But we don't cut corners here. We still experiment and invent our own equipment because we are interested in doing things differently. We do it because we're Disney.

—TOM FITZGERALD

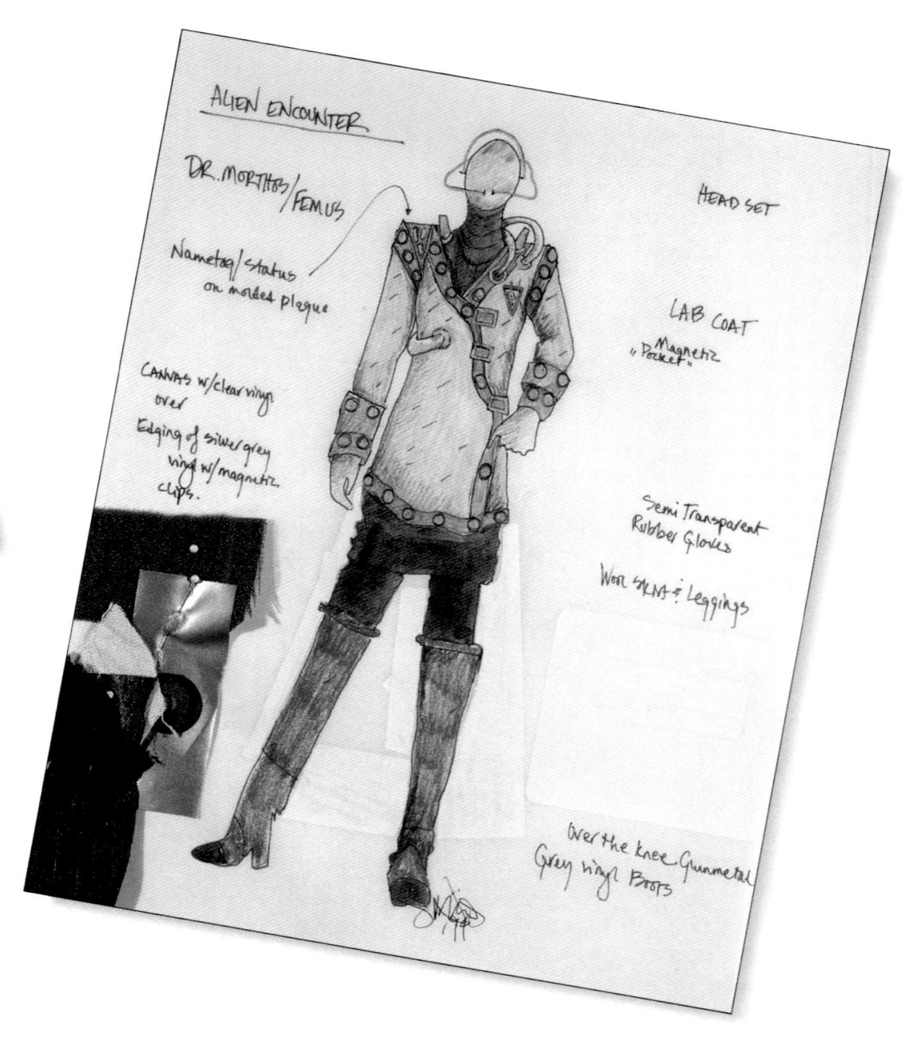

TOP: Playing two employees of a sinister intergalactic corporation, Kathy Najimy and Kevin Pollak prepare earthlings for a new technology demonstration that eventually goes awry in The ExtraTERRORestrial Alien Encounter in the Magic Kingdom at Walt Disney World.

ABOVE AND RIGHT: Design sketches (with sample fabric swatches) of the costumes worn by Spinlok (played by Kevin Pollak) and Dr. Femus (played by Kathy Najimy) in The ExtraTERRORestrial Alien Encounter.

LEFT: Honey, I Shrunk the Audience married the arts of filmmaking and special effects as never before, as the entire theater bounces and shakes its way through this amazing 3-D misadventure.

ABOVE: Artist George Stokes created this 1992 poster for Le Visionarium at Disneyland Paris, a comical time-travel journey led by your robotic guide, Timekeeper. Posters like these are an Imagineering tradition, helping convey the concept and story to guests who might not be familiar with the show—especially important in the multi-language environment of our world-wide parks.

RIGHT: Bill Nye takes Ellen DeGeneres "way back" to show her what we mean when we say "fossil fuels" in the Universe of Energy at Epcot.

BELOW: A huge primeval jungle set was created for "Ellen's Energy Crisis" inside one of Hollywood's largest soundstages.

We realize in order for our dreams to come true, change must be welcomed. There is nothing to fear, for when our vision remains fixed upon the goal, we know any path taken will lead us there.

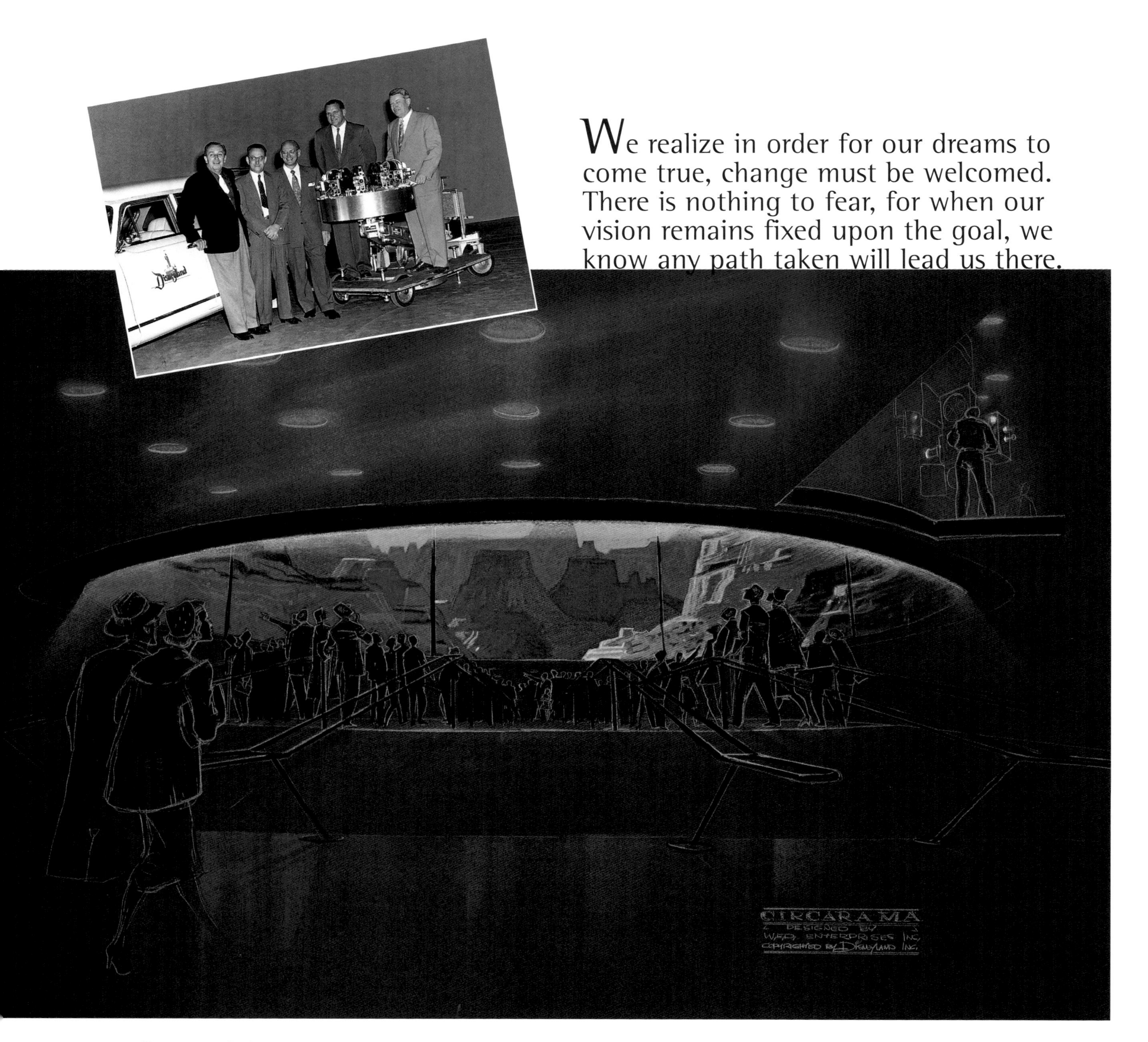

ABOVE: Since no one had ever seen or heard of a 360° movie theater, John Hench conceptualized what the amazing new "Circarama" experience might look like for Opening Day at Disneyland.

TOP: Walt Disney (left) shows off the first 360° camera rig—the "Circarama." In an attempt to outdo the popular wide-screen formats of the 1950s, Walt approached his camera experts and machine shop with the challenge of creating a 360° format. Their 16mm eleven-camera arrangement worked, but when the films were first projected "in the round," they caused eye strain and even dizziness. In his quest for perfection, Walt challenged his crew to eliminate this visual problem. The problem, it was discovered, was that because all the camera lenses faced outwards, they did not share exactly the same focal or nodal point. In order for the system to work properly, the cameras had to be aimed and focused at the same central nodal point. The problem was quickly remedied.

RIGHT: Walt Disney (second from left) inspects the second generation 360° camera mount. This version required only nine cameras (35mm), all focused into the same centralized focal point, which was a highly polished, angled mirror. The system worked flawlessly.

ABOVE AND LEFT: Circle-Vision camera rigs have traveled all over the world. Here the crew gets ready to shoot a breathtaking panorama during the filming of "Wonders of China."

BELOW: Our audio studios include the world's only 360° film "dubbing" stage. Here, Sam Buckner and Kurt Kinzel control a video-projected version of a Circle-Vision film in order to properly edit and mix the final "surround" sound track.

BOTTOM: American Journeys in Circarama makes its debut at Disneyland in 1984.

ABOVE: The scene is Mozart's 16th birthday party shot in Circle-Vision for Le Visionarium, a show in Disneyland Paris that, for the first time, was hosted by an Audio-Animatronics figure and featured in-theater effects. The figure is Timekeeper, the robot inventor of a time-traveling sidekick camera with an attitude named "9-Eye" whom he sends through time to transmit back an all-around view of history and the future. Unlike shooting a scene with one camera, where all you have to worry about is what appears in that one frame, a Circle-Vision rig sees everything. A set for an elaborate scene like this Mozart shot has to be built to work from every possible view. There can be no lighting fixtures, boom operators or directors just "out of frame," because in this case, *everything* is in "frame." And for every scene that has to be re-shot, each "take" requires nine cameras' worth of film!

Through all the blood, sweat, and tears, we have traveled upon many an unyielding road together. Defined and redefined, our idea has proven itself, and is now a single dream we all share. Still, it remains but a dream. Even more powerful than dreaming is making it real.

"People don't walk out of the attraction whistling the architecture."

–JOHN HENCH

IMAGINHEARING: AUDIO PRODUCTION

ABOVE: The Imagineering Video Library has cataloged 34,000 video tapes of Imagineering projects. Here, Jon Fisher prepares a tape transfer requested by one of the designers, one of more than 10,000 copies he has made since becoming an Imagineer.

ABOVE RIGHT: The Sherman Brothers—Robert, standing, and Richard, at the piano, composing the words and music for "It's a Small World" in 1963. From the Enchanted Tiki Room to the Carousel of Progress, The Sherman Brothers have composed more music for Imagineering projects than anyone else.

Imagine floating through Pirates of the Caribbean without hearing the warning, "Dead men tell no tales," or clapping your hands along with a bunch of silent Country Bears. Imagine Tarzan swinging right past you on a vine in the Great Movie Ride without his famous yell, or blasting upside-down in a Space Mountain rocket at Disneyland Paris without the on-board thrill-enhancing musical underscore. Sound—whether it be area background music, show underscore, dialogue or effects—is a vital story element in just about every Imagineering project.

From the haunting blast of the Big Thunder train whistle, to the happily chirping "birds" heard nearby along the banks of the Rivers of America (which, by the way, switches over at nightfall to chirping crickets and croaking frogs); from the "Peach Boys" singing the praises of good nutrition in Food Rocks at Epcot, to the memorable movie theme music heard all over the Disney-MGM Studios—in fact, every recorded sound you hear at any of our parks—was designed and produced at Imagineering. We maintain several state-of-the-art recording and production studios in our headquarters building where we record voice talent, entire orchestras, and full-blown sound effects.

Once scripted dialogue, musically orchestrated performances and sound effects are recorded, they are combined to build a digital show soundtrack. The process begins with editing the individual studio takes into a logical show sequence, then mixing the edited elements onto one multi-track configuration. The fully-assembled master soundtrack establishes the precise timing from which the entire show is programmed, including timing cues for all Audio-Animatronics figures, animated props, special effects and lighting.

Our in-house studios are equipped to produce the software required for final installation of a show. We can off-load a complete, fully mixed show from our computerized sound editor called an audiofile to make compact disks for general background music, or solid-state electronic chips, called E-Proms, which contain an entire show soundtrack. These can easily be

ABOVE: **Kurt Kinzel mixes the audio tracks for the Circle-Vision film at Le Visionarium. This custom-designed mixing panel can control as many as 400 separate audio channels at one time.**

ABOVE RIGHT: **Greg Meader engineers a recording session with "Sawdust," a musical group made up of Imagineers Alec Scribner, Steve Noceti, Steve Frankenberger and David Jones.**

ABOVE: **Media designer Glenn Barker plays the pots-and-pans "potaphonia" to create the sound effects for Minnie's Kitchen at Toontown.**

plugged into the show's main computer system.

In the early days, we recorded everything on 35mm motion picture film (called Mag Stripes). This was an ideal method for synchronizing sound with dimensional motion because film is divided into 24 frames-per-second, the same rate at which the Audio-Animatronics figures were recorded on tape. When the two were edited frame by frame, the narration, dialogue and music worked in precise synchronization with the dimensional animation (much like an animated film). The soundtrack, then, became the driver of the show. Pirates of the Caribbean, for example, used 112 soundtracks of this type to coordinate all of the figures, automated props, dialogue, lighting, special and sound effects. We have long since retired the 35mm format, and replaced it with state-of-the-art digital equipment.

Our sound studio becomes involved in a project when the concept team, with preliminary script in hand, is ready to determine sound requirements. The sound experts review both the script and the plans for the new attraction to determine what kinds of speakers should be acquired (or invented) and where they will be located. This also helps determine the number of soundtracks needed, including those that may be heard from directly inside a ride vehicle.

A sound effects designer working on a motion picture watches a rough version of the film several times to determine the types of effects required. The effects are then created and added to the film accordingly. An Imagineering sound effects designer must "ride" through an attraction several times (while it is still in the form of a storyboard and model) to determine the types of effects required, create the effects here at Imagineering, then ride through the actual attraction when it is nearly completed to fine-tune sound effects.

Now try to imagine what the show would be like while narrowly escaping the many dangers of the Indiana Jones Adventure, when suddenly, you round a bend only to find yourself trapped in a cavern by a giant boulder that is rolling and rumbling right towards you—without the rumble.

"It's our job to come up with sound solutions to creative ideas. We try to shoot for the moon. But we still have to keep it under control, because ultimately, it all has to be installed."

—GLENN BARKER
Audio Designer

How did you become an Imagineer?

Master Illusioneer Yale Gracey gets into the spirit of his work at the Haunted Mansion.

I was ten years old when the Haunted Mansion opened at Disneyland. Ever since it had been announced as a "future attraction," I had stared at the building with my face pressed against the iron fence, imagined what every inch of the inside was like, dreamed about it. The year it finally opened, Gulf Oil's Disney Magazine (distributed at gas stations) had a feature article about the Haunted Mansion. There was a photo of a scenic artisan carving a stone monument; he looks up from his hammer and chisel, startled, at the ghost of a wizened old king seated atop the monument, smiling down on him. This photo crystallized my career goal from the moment I saw it: someday I would be the guy in the smock, carving scenery for haunted mansions while ghosts oversaw my work.

Thenceforth I could be found during any school recess sitting at a lunch table, drawing and planning theme parks and attractions. My room filled with maps of Disneyland and homemade storyboards and models. As I grew older I studied art, animation and theater design. I finally started at Walt Disney Imagineering at 28, designing models for Disneyland Paris.

When people ask me, what qualified me to get hired at Imagineering? Where did I train? How does one prepare for a career as a theme park designer? I'm not sure how to respond. I feel like I've been an Imagineer since I was ten years old.

—DANIEL SINGER, Dimensional Design

"WHAT DID YOU DO AT WORK TODAY, HONEY?"

LEFT: Imagi-divers are immersed in their work to make sure Prince Eric's sailing ship is securely anchored in Storybook Land at Disneyland Paris.

BELOW: Sound effects wizard Joe Herrington is surrounded by many of the actual noise-making props that provided sounds to hundreds of live-action and animated Disney films by legendary studio sound effects man, and 38-year voice of Mickey Mouse, Jimmy Macdonald. Today, most film and theme park attraction sound effects are created digitally from a massive compact disk library of pre-recorded sounds. Sometimes, though, Joe finds that these old props still work best.

"I can't think of another design organization that covers all the bases we do—sculpture, sound, art, model building, train building, boat building. Each area plays off the next and produces a complete product that's all our own. We give things the Disney twist."

—BILL MARTIN

LEFT: Jenna Freré puts the finishing touches on a sarcophagus for the Great Movie Ride at the Disney-MGM Studios.

BELOW LEFT: Sculptors Valerie Edwards and Terry Izumi have created everything from theme park statuary to three-dimensional interpretations of concept sketches that will one day become Audio-Animatronics figures.

BELOW: Figure-finisher Michelle Wieczorek is as busy as a bee adding the final details to this giant prop for the Honey, I Shrunk the Kids "blue screen" show, part of the backstage tour at the Disney-MGM Studios.

BELOW: From foreground to rear, Sean Conway, Randy Meyers, Darrell Rohman and Rick Elliot get to work on Audio-Animatronics characters from the inside out.

ABOVE: Working on the scale model for Disneyland Paris, Olivia Ramirez, John Alexopolus and Charangsee Aiumopas will tell you they have model jobs.

RIGHT: Cyber Ace David Durham has a ball on his computer.

LEFT: Librarians Rick Hunt (seated) and Al Simpson lend their talents to the Information Research Center at Imagineering, home to more than 50,000 books and periodicals. The research center has been an invaluable source of information for Imagineering writers, architects, artists and designers for more than 30 years.

BELOW: Trinh Mai is putting the finishing touches on "9-Eye," the flying, talking camera character who sends 360° images from the past and future to Le Visionarium show at Disneyland Paris, and the Timekeeper show at the Magic Kingdom at Walt Disney World.

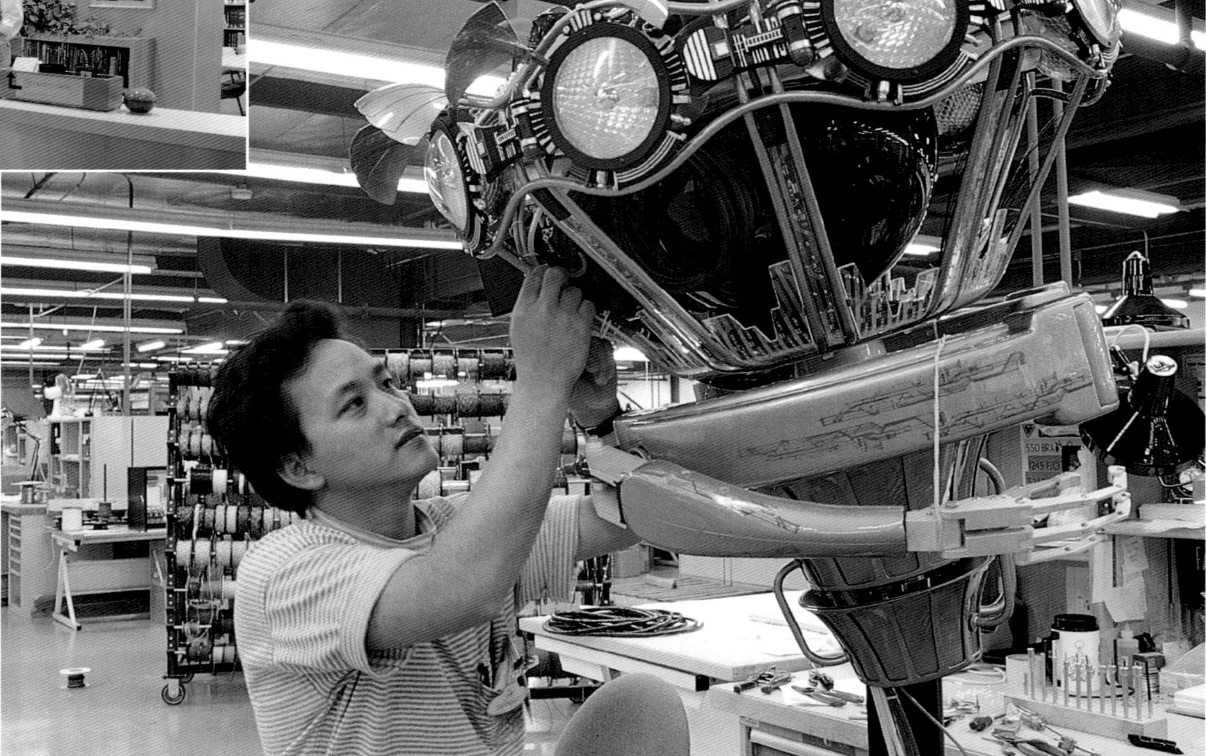

BELOW: Michelle Kilbourne stays focused on her work documenting Imagineering artwork.

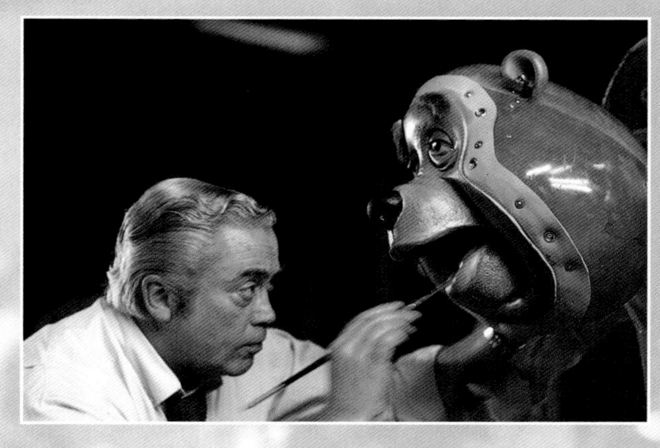

ABOVE: Big Al (right) opens wide for Ken O'Brien's paintbrush.

LEFT: Charting out a course for the Disney Cruise Lines are concept crew members Kris Wilhelm, Jim Durham, and Monica Gonzalez.

BELOW LEFT: Alfredo Ortega and David Tye demonstrate how being an Imagineer can be one of the sweetest jobs in the world.

ABOVE: Our support staff is the backbone of Imagineering. Here, Sally Judd and Billie Mendoza help to administer the magic.

LEFT: Adding the last piece to the model for the Alice In Wonderland Maze at Disneyland Paris are artists Dave Minichello and Vernon Terry.

BELOW: The magic begins for a new group of Imagineers as Human Resource Specialist Joan McLean conducts their orientation session.

RIGHT: Show Writers Pam Fisher, Art Verity and Melody Malmberg hit the books in the Information Research Center to help give an idea the write stuff.

BELOW RIGHT: Imagineering Sculptor Blaine Gibson faces his work head-on in the sculpture studio.

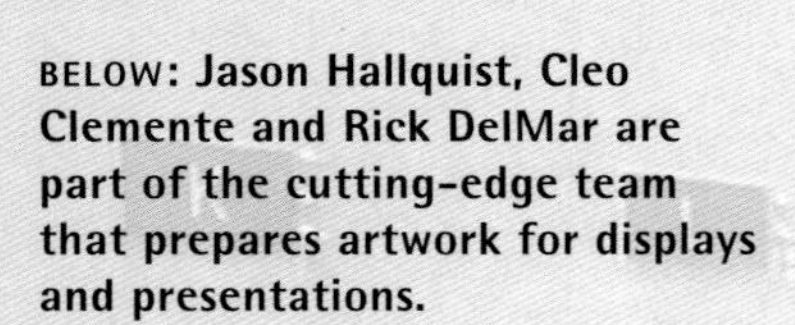

BELOW: Jason Hallquist, Cleo Clemente and Rick DelMar are part of the cutting-edge team that prepares artwork for displays and presentations.

LEFT: Marilyn Gage puts the final piece of steel in place on this structural scale model of Spaceship Earth.

LEFT: Architect Bill Mochidome and Interior Designer Steve Wilson concur over plans for the Tomorrowland Astrozone facility at Tokyo Disneyland.

BELOW: Hugh Chitwood, Diane Scoglio and Jill Centeno sort through some of the three million color slides and photographs in the Imagineering Slide Library. Included in the collection are storyboards, artwork, models, and complete documentation of the production and construction of every attraction Imagineering has ever created.

LEFT: Maintenance Engineer Mike O'Byrne ponders the age-old Imagineering question: does it have to be a light bulb?

BELOW: Gilles Martin air-brushes up on some of the finer details of model building.

ABOVE: Reviewing interior treatment samples and color boards designed for the Entertainment District at the Walt Disney World Village are John Ott, Jerry Parsey, Karen Klavens, Mike Merrill, and Frank Zork.

TOP: Burgin Dossett, Kha Le-Huu, and Jeanette Manent are preparing the "flight plan" for the whimsical airship seen in concept model form. The airship was designed as a themed show element for The World of Disney, the largest retail space at Walt Disney World.

BELOW LEFT: Denise Brown scans a computer barcode to catalog the location of one of more than 50,000 pieces of original art preserved in the Imagineering Art Library. In the background, Randy Webster and Joann Centeno retrieve a piece of artwork requested for review by one of the Imagineering designers.

BOTTOM LEFT: John Paul Bakshoian and Nancy Tarizzo check over the show documentation for a Disneyland restaurant. These binders—some of more than 3,000 that Show Documentation has prepared—provide detailed information about every show, merchandise shop and food facility in all the Disney parks.

BELOW RIGHT: Susan Toler has all the civil engineering facts and figures for Blizzard Beach down cold.

GETTING INTO OUR WORK

Unlike our colleagues in the television and film divisions, Imagineer's names do not appear in credits at the end of our shows. But sometimes, our initials do. We'll let you in on a little secret. Every once in a while we find fun and unusual ways to weave and leave our initials on a project. We don't make it a habit, mind you. Even if you look real hard, you won't find them often.

But every once in a while . . .

LEFT: Above Main Street at Disneyland Paris, this upstairs window suggests there are many fun things to discover on yet another level of the park.

ABOVE: Designed into the intricate iron scrollwork of New Orleans Square at Disneyland are the initials of our beloved founder.

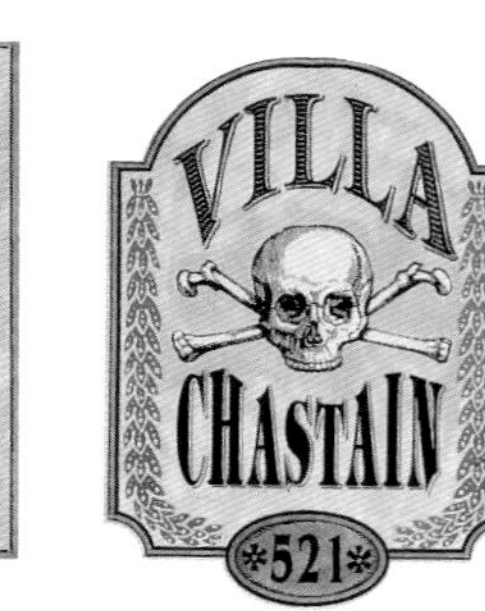

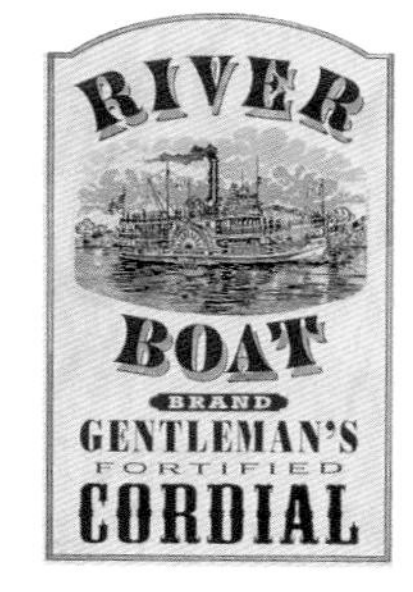

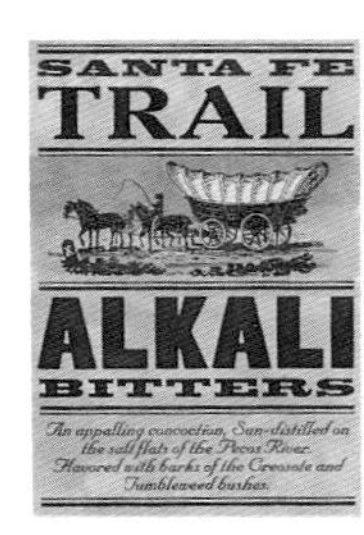

ABOVE: "X" marks the spot on this second-level window at Disneyland that pays tribute to one of Imagineering's most legendary artists and writers.

LEFT: These bottle labels were specially designed for the Graveyard scene in the Phantom Manor at Disneyland Paris. "Tujunga" and "Chastain" are better known as the names of two of our off-site Imagineering facilities.

ABOVE: Call it coincidence, but Imagineering is located on the same street as this one in Disneyland Paris!

BELOW: Those who know Audio-Animatronics pioneer Wathel Rogers may recognize his name on this Haunted Mansion headstone.

RIGHT: This fine restaurant above Main Street at Disneyland Paris took its name from a man who spent his childhood on a turn-of-the-century American street just like this one.

ABOVE: Imagineers exercised their creative license by including their initials and birth dates on license plates in the Sci-Fi Dine-In Restaurant at the Disney-MGM Studios.

LEFT AND BELOW: **Roger Broggie, Jr., Marc Davis, show writer Al Bertino and Bill Martin discuss the bear facts behind the character designs for Country Bear Jamboree. Marc Davis used Al as the inspiration for this bear-i-cature (left) for the Country Bear—and just like the real thing, this "Big Al" turned out to be one of our most memorable and beloved characters.**

REALLY GETTING INTO OUR WORK

Most Imagineers are real characters. And some of us find our way to being real characters in our shows and rides.

You may not realize it when you see or hear us, but sometimes we are there—whether it be a voice in Mickey's Toontown or an extra in Star Tours. Since we have our own production studios, every once in a while we'll use one of our talented crew and get fantastic results. This is what we call really getting into our work.

RIGHT: **When the crystal ball was being designed for the Seance Room in the Haunted Mansion, artist Leota Toombs (inset) was asked to play the role of the disembodied head as a temporary stand-in during a test of the effect—but she did such a great job that her temporary test became the final performance, and the character was named "Madame Leota" in her honor.**

LEFT: Senior Vice President (then Show Writer) Tom Fitzgerald lends his image and a hand to the Audio-Animatronics "Tom II," for Horizons at Epcot.

BELOW LEFT: Imagineers John Olson and Jeff Burke (standing) portrayed two brothers forced to fight against each other in the Civil War. This image was used for the "Two Brothers" sequence in the American Adventure at Epcot and in Great Moments with Mr. Lincoln at Disneyland.

ABOVE: Show designers Joe Lanzisero and Marcello Vignali clown around all day as caricatures in the Car Toon Spin attraction at Disneyland.

BELOW RIGHT: With the exception of a few of the furry ones, the passengers aboard this Star Tours StarSpeeder cabin (as seen in the boarding video) are all out-of-this-world Imagineers and their family members.

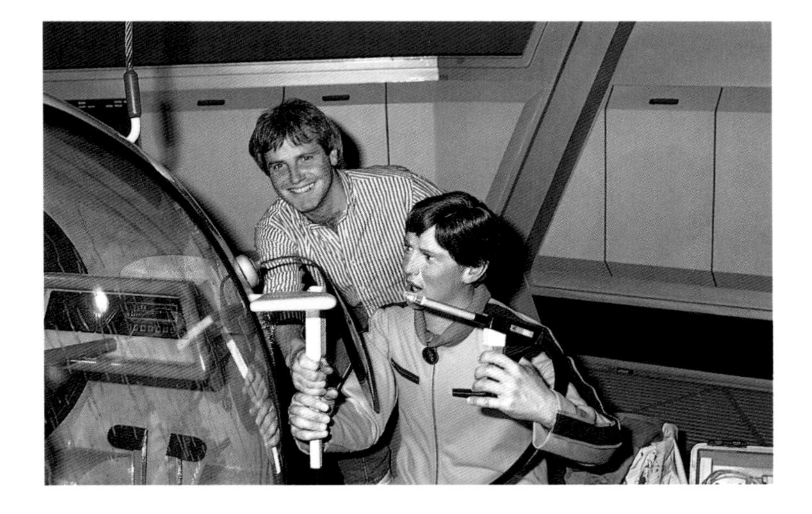

CHAPTER 4

MAKING IT REAL

"It's kind of fun to do the impossible."

—WALT DISNEY

RIGHT: **The vistas of the Grand Canyon bring the Old West to the Old World, in this mural being painted for the Grand Canyon Diorama at Disneyland Paris.**

OPPOSITE: **Cinderella Castle at Walt Disney World reaches closer to the sky, as its tallest spire is hoisted into place.**

It's time to put on our hard hats. Simultaneous efforts at the project site and at Imagineering are in high gear. Foundations are poured and structural frames are erected at the site while ride vehicles and animated figures and props are programmed and tested at Imagineering. Voice recordings, sound effects and music are being mixed into the final digital soundtracks while a construction crew whips up a batch of plaster to trowel onto the new facility.

At this point in our process, a show's support equipment, lighting fixtures, ride and audio systems—well, just about every piece of hardware—have been selected. Sets, props and set dressings are hand-fabricated at the Imagineering production facility in North Hollywood.

The core team that first ignited the spark of the project is busier than ever. They personally visit several locations on an ongoing basis, from the construction site to the off-site production facilities, from the recording studios to the graphics department. Eight-hour workdays and five-day work weeks are a faint memory. The team is living and breathing the project, fueled by opening day passion. This is an Imagineer's most frantic but most exciting time.

As the frenzy of activity continues, the core team answers last minute questions and addresses last minute changes. What was first envisioned in their heads and lovingly nurtured along on paper, in clay, cardboard and foam, is finally coming to life.

Once major construction is complete, all of the Imagineers involved in the project jump into the field to put the icing on the cake. Props, show sets, lighting fixtures, painted details, graphics, audio systems, projectors—everything that was once carefully considered from each Imagineering perspective—are delivered to the site like pieces of a puzzle to be carefully locked into place. Sometimes, hours, even minutes before opening, the last of the landscape materials are being tamped into place and paint is still being applied.

At last, the simple spark that first appeared on a crumpled lunch napkin has become a reality. The dream has finally come true. To the Imagineers who created it, the project has never felt more like a dream than it does on opening day. The feeling is pure magic.

Once we step onto the final path that ascends steeply towards reality, there is no turning back. We are encouraged onward by our belief in the dream, and each other. If it can be imagined, it can be believed. If it can be believed, it can be achieved!

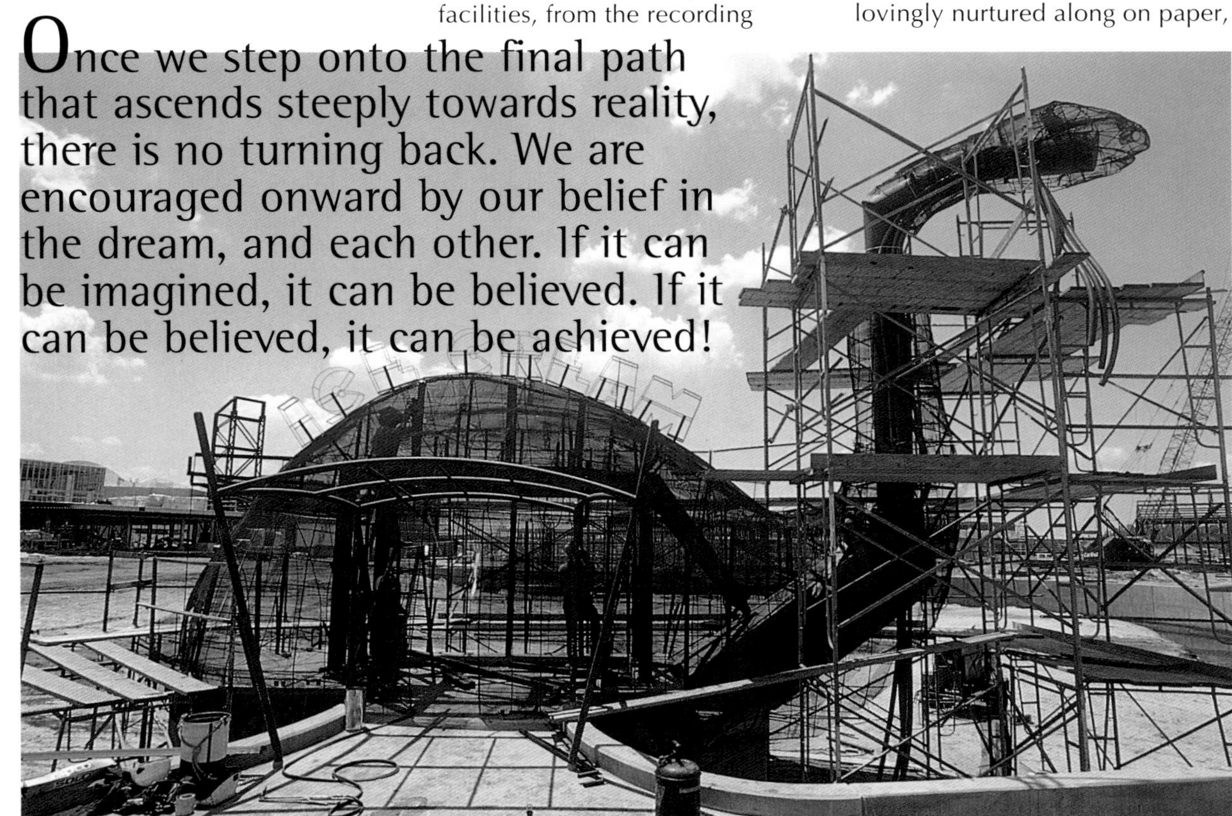

LEFT: **A steel-framed ice-cream stand at Disney-MGM Studios becomes a tribute to Gertie the Dinosaur the moment its framework is wrapped with sheets of carefully shaped metal lath. The real Gertie starred in the world's first animated film, Winsor McCay's "Gertie the Dinosaur." Once the framework has received its final coat of plaster, the stand will be ready to serve up its "Ice Cream of Extinction."**

"I'll never be able to work a normal job in this town again. And I don't mean Toontown!"

—Mickey's Toontown construction crew member

ABOVE AND OPPOSITE, LEFT TO RIGHT: A Goofy sequence of events begins with Joe Lanzisero's original concept sketch of "Goofy's House" for Toontown (which, at this early stage, was known as "Mickeyland"). The sketch is then visualized in three dimensions as a highly detailed scale model, which once again returns to two-dimensional form as an architectural drawing. Finally, the concept sketch, the model and the drawing are all used as reference to create the real house at Disneyland—an Imagineering process that any Goof would be proud of.

THE ANGLE ON MICKEY'S TOONTOWN

When construction workers first arrived on site and studied the building plans for Mickey's Toontown at Disneyland, they put their squares and levels back into their trucks. There were no right angles on the construction blueprints. There were no wrong angles either. The plans were exactly as we had intended. Tossing the traditional discipline of their craft to the wind, the construction crew glued plastic Mickey ears to their hard hats and set to work making real an unreal cartoon town. They actually had fun doing things the "wrong way," experimenting with their trades. Some were even heard to whistle while they worked.

Since the buildings were more sculptural than architectural, they were created like rockwork. But where steel cages that serve as the underlying structural frames for rockwork are normally computer designed and mechanically produced, they had to be handmade to accommodate all of the funny cartoon angles in Toontown. Using the drawings and models on-site, the concept team "eyeballed" the framework and directed the construction crew as to how to bend the steel framing, wire it all together to form structural cages, and trowel on the plaster base.

When the neighborhood of uncommon structures was nearing completion, each of the many show elements, including audio and visual media, lighting fixtures, graphics, 2,100 purchased props, 958 made-from-scratch props (including "cartoonized" picture frames, books, garbage cans, light switches and faucet heads) were brought to the site and put into place. Despite the abandonment of T-squares, levels and logic, everything fit like a glove.

"Because of its cartoon nature, it was actually better when a window was cut wrong. At first it was difficult to get the workers to understand that. When they installed a door, they would ask, 'do you want it to hang straight?' And our response would be, 'Of course not. Crooked is more toony.'"

—DAVE BURKHART, Project Management

RIGHT: There's not a right angle anywhere in sight, as Minnie's House rises in the residential section of Toontown.

"There is a flow and rhythm to this land you won't find anywhere else. All of the architectural elements follow certain lines, none of which are straight. Everything has a strong internal logic that makes sense, but it can only make sense in Toontown."

—JOE LANZISERO, Concept Design

BELOW: The almost completed Goofy's House rises above downtown Toontown, as the project rapidly approaches opening day.

LEFT: Giant blades of grass loom 30 feet overhead in Richard Vaughn's concept sketch for the Honey I Shrunk the Kids Movie Set Adventure at Disney-MGM Studios.

ABOVE AND BELOW: The happiness of our guests is usually nothing to sneeze at—except in the case of this delightful concept by Greg Wilzbach. The vapor that sprays from the giant dog nose may seem real, but it's not!

OPPOSITE: The steel structures of the Honey I Shrunk the Kids Movie Set Adventure are in place, waiting for the arrival of the giant sets and props.

OPPOSITE INSET: The finished movie set towers above the adjacent buildings.

"I think we put more steel in those grass stalks than the Eiffel Tower and the Statue of Liberty combined. There's a gas inside the blade armatures to make sure there are no structural stresses or leaks in the welds, and there's an electronic reading device to make sure there are no cracks. This is really high-tech grass."

—MICHAEL McGIVENEY, Show Production

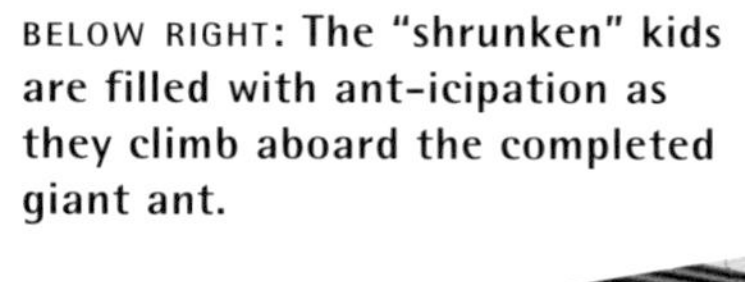

BELOW LEFT: Imagineers Jimmy Thomas (left) and Ed Mason get a leg up on the project as they assemble a giant ant for the Honey I Shrunk the Kids Movie Set Adventure.

BELOW RIGHT: The "shrunken" kids are filled with ant-icipation as they climb aboard the completed giant ant.

Honey, I Blew Up the Theme Park Attraction

Shortly after the Disney-MGM Studios opened in Florida, we decided to add a children's playground. It certainly couldn't be just an average play area. It would have to allow guests to experience what it is like to be "shrunk" to the size of an ant and journey through a giant backyard—just as do the stars of the motion picture, *Honey, I Shrunk the Kids.*

Creating and designing the play area was relatively easy as we based it on recreating the movie set. But a movie set is not intended to be played upon, nor is it intended to last even beyond the shooting of a scene. Building this "big idea" took some large-scale thinking.

The Honey, I Shrunk the Kids Movie Set Adventure—which includes 45 stalks of 30-foot-high grass, a 16-foot-tall building block and a 52-foot-long garden hose (attached to a nozzle that squirts real water)—was constructed to withstand outdoor elements along with the daily hands-on activity from thousands of guests. Most importantly, it was built to be safe.

Everything within the play area is softened to eliminate hard edges. All of the pathways are coated with rubber, and the individual elements, such as a giant piece of cereal, a giant dog nose, an ant and ferns are made with a foam-based surface that is covered with urethane. The enclosed slides are made of pliable polyethylene. The grass stalks, each supporting two to three 28-foot blades of grass, are supported by 500 pounds of structural steel to withstand fierce 80-mile-an-hour winds. Prior to installation, each was tested in a wind tunnel at Cal Tech.

Today, kids of all ages enjoy exploring this larger-than-life movie set without giving much thought to all of the safety considerations that went into its construction. But that's the big idea.

GETTING IT THERE IS HALF THE FUN

If you're ever driving down the road and the trunk that's on the vehicle in front of you is not the rear part of a car—but the front part of an elephant—you're probably following an Imagineering show element being delivered to the site.

Because most of our projects are so unusual, they contain show elements that are custom-made at either our Glendale or North Hollywood facility, sort of like making a ship in a bottle. Whether it's a large set, prop, oversized Audio-Animatronics figure or ride vehicle, they are all designed and fabricated here at "home." Once they are assembled and detailed, and meet the approval of the show team, the show elements are tested to make sure they perform as designed. Having passed the test, they are disassembled, packed up and shipped for installation to one of our theme parks somewhere in the world. In most cases, an overnight delivery package just won't do!

On one memorable occasion, during last-minute show installation for the Magic Kingdom at Walt Disney World, one of the Audio-Animatronics human figures was accidentally left behind in a crate on the North Hollywood facility loading dock as the loaded truck pulled out for Florida. In order to accommodate the tight opening day schedule, the female figure was unpacked, dressed in a nice business suit and given a passenger ticket on a commercial airline. She enjoyed a window seat next to her traveling companion, one of the Imagineers en route to Florida. Wearing sunglasses, airline headphones and a large hat, she hardly touched her in-flight meal and "read the newspaper" all the way to Orlando.

Motorists are generally used to seeing large trucks carrying cars, heavy machinery and the like, but when they were following a truckload of giant toys from the Toy Story Action Adventure set heading down the Santa Ana Freeway in the general direction of Disneyland, it made most of them look twice. It's all part of putting a show together—and taking it on the road!

BELOW: The menacing hippopotamus hitches a ride on his way to the Jungle Cruise.

BELOW: Captain Nemo's submarine *Nautilus* comes to the surface in 1971 as it travels through Downtown Orlando on its way to the Magic Kingdom at the Walt Disney World Resort.

ABOVE: A plastic-wrapped giant Stegosaurus begins its long journey from California to New York for the 1964–1965 World's Fair. When the Fair closed in 1965, the Stegosaurus returned to Disneyland, where it can still be found battling a Tyrannosaurus Rex in the Primeval World along the route of the Disneyland Railroad.

BACKGROUND: "Big Squirt" arrives at Disneyland, on his way to the Elephant's Bathing Pool in Adventureland.

You know what you haven't got?

In the early days at Disneyland, not all the technology introduced was geared towards the future. Sometimes Imagineers got to recreate a classic piece of technology from the past. No matter the subject, they knew they would be developing another one of Walt's new ideas whenever he would approach them, slap his knee and say, "Hey, you know what we haven't got?" After he filled them in on the new idea, the studio accounting department would call them with the go-ahead.

ABOVE: Bob Gurr's spark for a Main Street fire truck caught fire once Walt gave him the go-ahead. This is the design from which the truck was actually built.

One day, a young Imagineer named Bob Gurr turned the tables on Walt with one of his own ideas, saying (knee slap), "Hey Walt, you know what we haven't got? A fire truck!" Bob stood there waiting for a response from Walt, but only got a raised eyebrow. Dejected, he went back to his office. A few moments later, his phone rang. It was the accounting department giving him the go-ahead.

Bob soon had the classic fire truck designed and built. It was a hand-made gleaming red beauty with a twelve-horsepower, two-cylinder engine. Even though it was designed to travel slowly up and down Main Street, Bob decided to drive the fire truck from the Studio in Burbank to Disneyland, about 35 miles. Since the truck could not keep up with the flow of traffic, he drove it as close to the right-hand side of the street as possible to allow cars to pass. Putt-putting down the road, he spotted a young boy running alongside and heard him call out, "Hey, mister, by the time you get there, it'll be burned down!"

BELOW: The Moonliner rocket ship arrives in Tomorrowland in 1955, ready to be hoisted onto its launching pad. The Moonliner would tower above Tomorrowland for more than a decade, taking guests on an imaginative "Flight to the Moon."

We have taken the tiny spark of an idea on a long journey that is nearing the end. But this ending is truly a beginning as we prepare the dream for a reality that exists beyond paper, canvas, and clay. The spark—our long-tended seed—is ready to rise up to touch the sky!

Building the Dream

"While we were finishing Disneyland Paris, there was a long period when it was so cold the paint would literally freeze on the brush before you could get it on the walls. We put up tents against the buildings and got some portable heaters so we could keep working in that bitter cold. We even roasted weenies on the heaters because they had big flames. Everyone else thought we Americans were crazy. But we didn't quit until it was done."

—KATIE OLSON, Show Design

ABOVE: "X" marked the spot where Cinderella's Castle would soon stand in the Magic Kingdom. From left to right, Marty Sklar, Dick Irvine, and Welton Beckett survey the Disney World–famous site in October 1967.

TOP RIGHT: Walt Disney gets his very own Matterhorn Mountain, as this 1/100th-scale replica rises above Disneyland in 1959.

BACKGROUND: Le Chateau de la Belle au Bois Dormant—that's "Sleeping Beauty Castle" to the rest of us—rises high above Disneyland Paris as the park nears completion in 1992.

ABOVE: Craftsmen put the finishing touches on the submarine *Nautilus*, in Discoveryland at Disneyland Paris. Despite its riveted and bolted steel-plated appearance, the submarine is actually built entirely out of cement.

ABOVE: The mythology of Typhoon Lagoon recounts the tale of a giant wind storm that left Miss Tilly perched high and dry up on top of the hill—but here the truth is finally revealed!

Shovels are turning in a passionate yearning for earth to meet our dream. Soon, we begin to manifest the idea in brick, mortar, steel, glass, wood, and paint. When the elements are assembled in a magical place, they define the shape of enchantment. They build the dream.

OPPOSITE, TOP LEFT: Sleeping Beauty Castle at Disneyland—the first, the smallest and perhaps the most charming of all the Disney castles—nears completion in the summer of 1955.

OPPOSITE, TOP RIGHT: The Swiss Family Treehouse towers more than 80 feet above the waters surrounding Adventure Isle at Disneyland Paris. To the Imagineers it's known as the Disneyodendren semperflorens grandis (the large, everblooming Disney tree), and is one of only four such trees known to exist in the entire world.

OPPOSITE: The 180-foot tall geodesic sphere of Spaceship Earth is carefully assembled one piece at a time during the construction of Epcot in 1981. In the foreground, a single section of the monorail beam has been left uninstalled to provide an opening where the giant cranes can be driven off the construction site. The last crane out set the final beam in place.

ABOVE: The steel framework for the giant Tree of Life begins to "grow" in the Animal Kingdom at the Walt Disney World Resort. When complete, the tree will tower more than 13 stories above the park.

BELOW LEFT: Discovering "Hidden Mickeys" throughout the Disney parks has become a popular activity for guests—almost as popular as hiding the Mickeys has become for Imagineers. Here we see a very Egyptian Donald Duck presenting an offering of cheese to Mickey, in a mural tucked away in the background of . . . well, we can't make it too easy!

BELOW RIGHT: Unexpected conditions often arise during the actual construction process which require immediate on-the-spot solutions from the Imagineering designers. Here, John Stone creates a quick sketch to help the construction crews working on Splash Mountain at Disneyland visualize exactly what the revised scene will look like when it's complete.

TAKING IT FOR GRANITE

ABOVE TOP, MIDDLE, AND BOTTOM:
While real rocks are formed by nature's forces, rockwork found at our theme parks takes a little Disney magic. Show Designers work from renderings to develop rockwork models, which are built by Production Designers. The models are physically cut up into workable size construction units. Upon each module is drawn a detailed X, Y and Z grid which represents the structural steel bars, called "rebar," that will eventually support the rockwork. Absolute accuracy is required, so a digitizer such as the one being used here by Betsy Webb captures the shape of each line. A computer converts this information into calculations that actually drive an automatic rebar bending machine. The final product is a full-size piece of bent rebar which is assembled to create a full-size construction unit, or rebar cage. The final full-size cage is identical in shape and detail to the original scale model.

Creating outside show environments is not just limited to architecture and themed landscaping. Some of our finest shows have been created by simulating rocks and mountains. Re-creating a natural setting is difficult; creating a fantasy setting that must appear to be natural is even harder. That is where well-executed rockwork—a fine art in itself—comes into the picture.

Unlike a film crew that can shoot on location, we have to bring the location to us. If our story calls for a mountain covered with snow smack dab in the middle of Florida, then we have to create one.

But rockwork is not usually executed for appearance alone. Often its infrastructure houses or supports all or part of an attraction—such as Splash Mountain, the Matterhorn or Big Thunder Mountain—as well as communicating a natural setting and theme. In the early days of rock simulation, as Imagineers were experimenting with and developing the art, the interior cages (structural steel frames formed in the shape of the rockwork) were bent by hand in the nearest parking lot. Today, the cages are designed on computer, and the steel is automatically bent by an Imagineering-patented machine.

If the vision of the dream evolving into reality holds steadfast to the vision of our concept, it seems more like a dream than ever before—it is a dream come true!

Simulating rock is not a common job. For rockwork to be successful, every inch of it must be done right. Bad rockwork immediately calls attention to itself as being something unnatural. Good rockwork, no matter what the style and theme, seems natural and is pleasing to the eye. With the exception of the major mountain-themed attractions, many of our guests assume that much of the rockwork in our parks was always there, part of the natural landscape. And that is fine with us, because if you take our simulated rockwork for granite, we are doing our job.

ABOVE: One of the most exciting moments of any project—the "topping off" ceremony, when the highest piece of the structure is installed. Here, Br'er Fox's tree stump (adorned with a Disney flag) is hoisted high atop Chickapin Hill at the top of Splash Mountain, in the Magic Kingdom at the Walt Disney World Resort.

RIGHT: With a final coat of scenic paint, even the most fanciful rockwork structures can be brought to convincing life. Here, we see a forest of giant mushrooms and carrots in the underground caverns of Splash Mountain at Disneyland—all created out of metal lath and cement!

"We landscaped all of Disneyland in less than a year with a maximum of arm waving and a minimum of drawings."

—BILL EVANS, Landscape Design

"In the year before Disneyland opened, you just couldn't escape Walt. He toured the place daily. After I finished planting a pepper tree beside the Plaza Pavilion Restaurant, Walt walked by and made a comment in passing that it was a little too close to the curb. So I moved all ten tons of it a little ways back. The next day he walked by and didn't say a word. He just smiled."

—BILL EVANS, Landscape Design

THE LANDSCAPE OF DREAMS

Long before ground is broken for construction, specific plant materials are cast to play a role as characters in the story.

The easiest way to cast a plant or tree is to select a species that can perform effectively in all kinds of climates, such as one that can play a desert role as effectively as it can play in a tropical jungle scene. But it is not always that easy. A plant material is selected only if it appears authentic to the theme of the scene—even if it is not native to the intended location. The plants must beat the odds and survive in climates and soil foreign to their zone of origin. An olive tree—not native to Florida—was sent from the dry Mediterranean region to play a role at the Italy Pavilion at Epcot. North American Sequoias were sent to Disneyland Paris to play a role in Frontierland.

Many plants and trees found along the shores of the three versions of the Jungle Cruise, located in three different parts of the world, are native to the jungles of Africa and South America. Many of the species not indigenous to Japan, but planted at Tokyo Disneyland anyway, were not expected to survive. Strangely enough, the Japanese Jungle Cruise somehow developed its own ecosystem and is doing splendidly. As soon as the winter snow melts at Tokyo Disneyland, you will find a lush tropical jungle.

The landscape at Disneyland is 90 percent non-indigenous to California. Many of its more than 800 species of plants and trees are actually native to Australia, Mexico, Europe and Asia. Except for a botanical garden, Disneyland, in fact, features the largest collection of plant species found anywhere in the world.

Outside the world of Disney, the typical landscape or area development plan follows the design of a building. Space is allotted for its eventual installation, but types of landscape materials are not even considered until after construction is completed.

We do just the opposite at Imagineering. Our landscape plan is designed concurrent with the development of an overall idea, never as an afterthought. Every aspect and detail of our area development—which includes everything outside a building, such as plant materials, walkways, bridges, waterways and lakes—is identified far in advance. Specific seedlings are planted at a tree farm to get things going, and certain species of established trees—authentic to the concept theme—are found in locations all over the world and stored until ready for transplant. Once construction nears completion, each of these members of the landscape cast arrives on the scene to take its place on stage.

ABOVE: The first Imagineer to begin the process of theme park landscaping was Bill Evans, shown here with one of the nursery owners who provided the original planting materials for Disneyland. In 1954, after Bill had completed the landscape design and installation at Walt Disney's home, Walt asked him if he would be interested in landscaping Disneyland. Bill has been "casting" landscape roles in our parks ever since.

BELOW: Flowers bring the world of the future to life outside The Land at Epcot.

"What do you mean we can't get rid of those weeds in time? Then go over there and put some fancy signs with Latin names in front of them."

—WALT DISNEY

TOP LEFT AND RIGHT, ABOVE, AND LEFT: **There wasn't much landscaping left once the orange groves were cleared away from the Disneyland site in 1954. Four decades later, Mother Nature (with a little help from the Imagineers) had provided the missing scenery along the Rivers of America in Frontierland and the Rivers of the World in Adventureland.**

"We love to research new plant materials and grow them where they've never been grown before. Right now, we're testing twelve different species of trees that have never been outside Japan. Our new technologies are helping them flourish in Florida and California."

—BERJ BEHESNILIAN, Landscape Design

RIGHT: **Forty years after the opening of Disneyland, landscape artist Bill Evans lovingly tends an exotic tree in Future World at Epcot—one of the many non-native species of plants he has successfully imported to Disney parks in Florida, Tokyo and Paris. Bill's talents have made it possible for the Imagineers to create everything from jungles to deserts, half-way around the world from where those environments would normally be found.**

THESE PAGES: **Careful attention to detail at all levels is one of the most important tools the Imagineers use to tell their stories, as seen in these views of Mexico (above) and Morocco (right) at Epcot Center, and Cinderella Castle (below) in the Magic Kingdom at the Walt Disney World Resort.**

LAYERS OF DETAIL: FROM LONG SHOT TO CLOSE-UP

When you walk through a Disney theme park, you experience the movie-making techniques of the long shot and the close-up. As you step into our parks, your sense of horizon is diminished as we first focus your attention on the long shots. Soon, your eyes detect splashes of color that begin to define neatly organized shapes. This simple tool establishes the scene and creates the illusion that ahead lies something entirely different, even better than that which you saw only a moment before. Stepping near enough to an object or building to see and define its shape, color and *detail*, is the close-up.

Imagineering Senior Vice President John Hench recalls a time prior to the opening of Disneyland when he tried to talk Walt out of wanting to put so much detail on a stagecoach. "Why don't we just leave the leather straps off, Walt?" John questioned. "The people are never going to appreciate all this close-up detail." Walt turned, firmly planted his finger on John's chest, and replied, "You're being a poor communicator. People are okay, don't you ever forget that. They will respond to it. They will appreciate it." Walt had come to know his audience. "Walt genuinely liked people," added John. "There was nothing cynical about him. Perhaps that is why he wanted so badly to communicate his stories to them. He just wanted to make them happy. We put the best darned leather straps on that stagecoach you've ever seen."

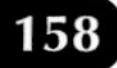

There is nothing like completing the inch-by-inch climb towards the summit that rises high above all clouds of doubt. It takes all of us, standing shoulder to shoulder and working closely together, to pass the flag of accomplishment all the way up to the top.

An illuminating touch

When most people consider Disney lighting, they usually think about how our parks take on a different, even magical appearance after the sun goes down. Lighting is a key show element for everything outdoors, as well as for everything indoors.

Each of our shops, restaurants and attractions would be an entirely different kind of experience under the evenly distributed glow of normal, non-theatrical overhead lights.

Things we may not necessarily want you to see, such as backstage areas and support equipment, would be exposed. To capture your attention, we create focus by directing sources of light only in the areas and on the objects we want you to see. A great majority of the drama and adventure created along the way is accomplished thanks to a well thought-out and executed theatrical lighting plan.

Like other interrelated show elements such as music and effects, lighting is a powerful tool used to evoke a certain mood or feeling. Light can sharply define as well as it can soften. It can whisper intimacy as well as shout surprise. Each fixture can be computer programmed to come on, fade up, ramp down or fade out where most appropriate. That is why, as the story for an attraction evolves, so too does an intricate plan for lighting it—both inside and out. Lighting design—which includes outdoor area development lighting, behind-the-scenes programmable show lighting and themed on-stage character fixtures—is a vital part of every project we do.

A lighting designer at Imagineering becomes part of the show team during the early stages of concept development. He or she comes into a project, not just to establish the lighting requirements, but to shed new light on other aspects of the idea along with other members of the team.

INSET PHOTOS: **When night falls, Tomorrowland in the Magic Kingdom at the Walt Disney World Resort is transformed into a kinetic world of glowing neon, as orchestrated by lighting designer Michael Valentino.**

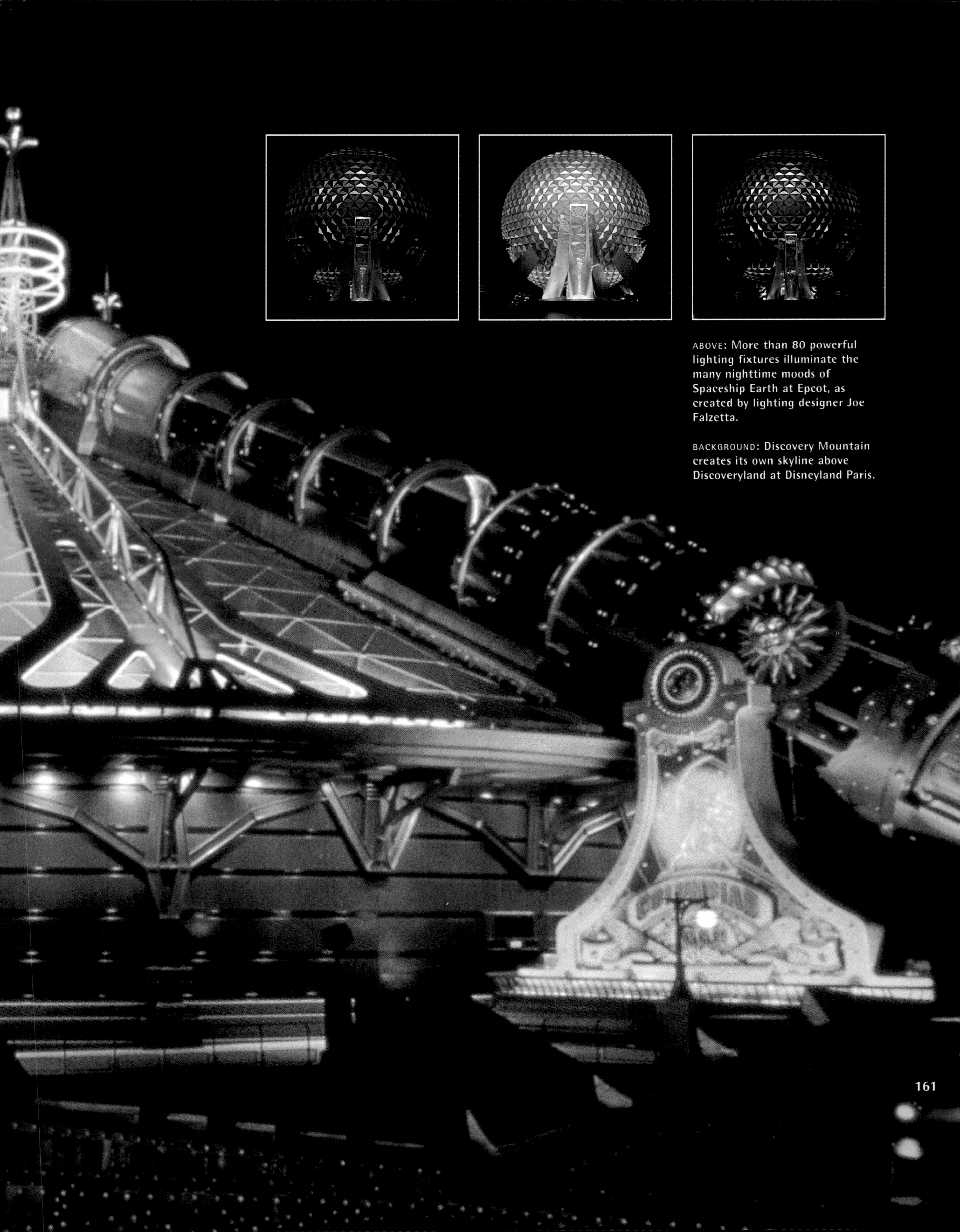

ABOVE: More than 80 powerful lighting fixtures illuminate the many nighttime moods of Spaceship Earth at Epcot, as created by lighting designer Joe Falzetta.

BACKGROUND: Discovery Mountain creates its own skyline above Discoveryland at Disneyland Paris.

THE HOLLYWOOD TOWER

"A lot of people have told me they don't remember a Twilight Zone *episode about an elevator. And they're right. This is the 'lost episode' no one has ever seen."*

—MICHAEL SPROUT, Show Writing

NEXT STOP, THE DESIGN ZONE . . .

Witness, if you will, the evolution of an idea for a thrill ride that began with an attempt to build an attraction themed around a free-falling ride system. Because the attraction was intended for the Disney-MGM Studios, its theme had to reflect movies or television.

The first idea on the sketch pads pictured a run-down Hollywood hotel that guests would walk through—an experience that culminates in some kind of haunted elevator experience. The first-pass story for the big idea was based on a Film Noir-style murder mystery: While throwing a big studio wrap party, the hotel owner went berserk and murdered his guests, one by one, before escaping in the elevator. But management killed the murder angle before it even made it to a storyboard.

The next story idea involved a group of movie stars filming a horror picture who all stayed at this hotel during production, but mysteriously disappeared one stormy night after boarding the elevator. The proposed walk-through, to be narrated by Vincent Price, provided guests clues along the way that eventually revealed how the movie stars disappeared—but by then the guests would be aboard the elevator and it would be too late.

After seeing this concept, Michael Eisner felt the idea needed a stronger story hook, and wanted our guests to somehow play a part in the story. In response, the concept team came up with the idea that guests could play roles as actors in their own episode of the *Twilight Zone*.

The team created mythology to support this idea. Something strange happened at this abandoned yet stately hotel—a one-time gathering place for the social elite—during Hollywood's heyday in 1939. One dark and stormy night, at the precise moment the elevator doors closed on two glamorous movie stars, a bellhop, and a budding young child star and her governess, a bolt of lightning struck the hotel's tower with such a force that it caused the five passengers to disappear. After the horrible event, the hotel lost all its clientele and was forced to close its doors.

The team wanted the tone and atmosphere of the attraction to make guests feel as if they had physically stepped into an episode of the *Twilight Zone* television show. The experience was designed in this sequence: Guests enter the aged, dust-blanketed lobby left untouched for more than five decades—until now. Suitcases and steamer trunks remain unchecked beside the front desk and martinis remain half-full on tables. A sign on the elevator proclaims it "Out of Order." As these "new" guests progress into the hotel library, the room darkens, lightning flashes, and a television mysteriously clicks on. Appearing on the old-style screen is Rod Serling, who delivers the introduction to their episode while setting up the unusual tale about the hotel and its elevator.

Directed down into the creepy boiler room, guests soon discover a freight elevator—rusted inoperable until now. Its doors open wide, ready to take a trip up to the uncharted 13th floor. If they so dare, they step inside, hoping lightning does not strike in the same place twice. But, of course, it does. . .

This version of the story was approved. Like the *Twilight Zone*, there were plenty of mysteries that had to be solved on the way to making it real. Some of the biggest challenges were confronted by the special effects team, who had to actually take guests into the Twilight Zone. But the greatest unknown was the ride system itself. How do you build an elevator that stops at a few floors while going up, breaks free from the shaft to travel horizontally across the floor, then enters into another shaft to drop freely straight down—all in perfect orchestration with the other show elements? After briefly considering actual elevator hardware, it was quickly determined that this particular system would have to be designed from the ground up.

After several generations of evolving designs, the final system exceeded all expectations. To make the ride even more exciting than a mere free-fall, the system was designed to thrust the elevator cars down so they would travel even faster than the force of gravity.

To accomplish this feat, Imagineering created the world's largest ride system motors to power the tandem vehicles. Twelve feet tall, 7 feet wide, 35 feet long and weighing in at 132,000 pounds, the two massive motors had to be hoisted atop the tower's framework—specially constructed to support their weight—via giant construction cranes.

The motors are capable of accelerating ten tons at a rate of fifteen times the speed of a normal elevator while generating torque equal to that of a combined 275 Corvette engines. At the show's finale, when the elevator takes its exhilarating plunge, it reaches top speed in less than 1.5 seconds, then comes to a smooth, complete stop all within a distance of 130 feet.

But Imagineering cannot take all the credit for such a ride system. An elevator like this can only be found in . . . the Twilight Zone.

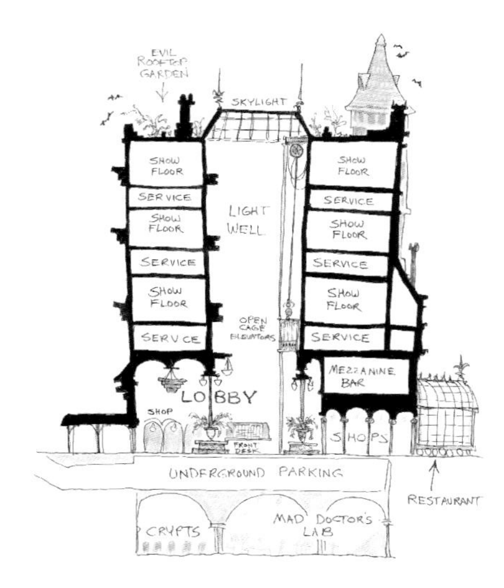

ABOVE: Tim Kirk created this early cut-away concept sketch to illustrate how the show might fit into the hotel's twin towers.

TOP RIGHT: The Tower of Terror towers above Sunset Boulevard, in this 1992 sketch by concept architect Coulter Winn.

OPPOSITE: A massive bolt of lightning strikes the Hollywood Tower Hotel in 1939 and launches it into the Twilight Zone, in this 1992 conceptual rendering by R. Tom Gilleon.

The
HOLLYWO D TOWER
Hot'l

WE FELL FOR IT

During the concept development of the runaway elevator thrill ride The Twilight Zone Tower of Terror, the core team decided to begin the project by drawing on the expertise of the Otis Elevator Company. Otis invited the team to visit a new high-rise building in Los Angeles where they had just completed installation of their fastest generation elevator. The team was anxious to give it a try since, above all, the ride had to be fast.

Dropping from the fiftieth floor, even after Otis had adjusted the elevator to "full speed," the team found themselves quickly at ground level without feeling a thing. "So what did you think?" asked an Otis executive. "It's fast, all right," responded a concept team member, "but what we were really looking for is a gut-wrenching, hair-raising, free-falling thrill!" To that, the surprised executive responded, "What? And undo everything we've been trying to perfect for more than a century? Our success comes when you feel like you're not moving at all!"

It was then the team realized how incredibly different this new elevator would have to be—and that it would be up to Imagineering to take it to a whole new level.

Like the untried wings of a butterfly emerging from its cocoon, our dream is at last unfolding into reality. And like that new butterfly, the dream is now ready to fly, because its wings have opened wide enough to touch the magic.

ABOVE LEFT: This mixed-media "cutaway" of the Twilight Zone Tower of Terror is actually a single-panel storyboard designed by Phillip Freer, which was used during early project development as a means of presenting the unusal ride and story sequence to management.

BELOW LEFT: The Tower of Terror was designed and refined until the final configuration was agreed upon, as seen in this scale model created by Wayne Robinson and Gary Moyer.

OPPOSITE: Night falls over the Twilight Zone, as the completed Tower of Terror rises majestically and ominously above the Disney-MGM Studios.

INSIDE OF FOLDOUT: Guests brave enough to experience the Twilight Zone suddenly find themselves plunging 130 feet from the top of the tower to the basement below—falling even faster than the force of gravity—as seen in this rendering by Nina Rae Vaughn.

ABOVE: As construction begins on the Tower of Terror, steel and concrete rise to a height of 199 feet.

"The breakthrough came when we stopped treating the system like an elevator and started treating it like a ride. Then we went for the max."

—CHRIS OLIVER, Ride Systems

"Walt Disney dreamed of a place where families could go to have fun together—a place of fantasy and magic. Disneyland was the first of many such places and Imagineering is where the real magic is created. I believe it is the most magical organization in the world."

—MICHAEL D. EISNER

The blanket of snow adding the final touch of magic to this fairytale-like scene in front of Cinderella Castle at Tokyo Disneyland is not a special effect. When it comes to setting the perfect scene, it's hard to beat Mother Nature.

CHAPTER 5

THE MAGIC

Before our eyes the tiny spark of an idea has grown into something magical!

Well, we've come to the end of our project story. Or have we? Actually, it is only the beginning because starting now, and for decades to come, our guests can share in our dream. Sustained by art, words, risk, passion, engineering, architecture, sharing, caring and (mostly) contagious enthusiasm, our dream has at long last come true.

As in every Disney tale, the idea experienced quite an adventurous journey, from dreaming the impossible dream to bravely conquering all obstacles. Since that first what if, the project has had to overcome Mount Everest-sized mountains of "blank sheets of paper," but any Imagineer will tell you it was well worth the climb

But wait just a minute. There is more to it than meets the eye. It is what meets the heart that is always the best part of any story. You see, the very moment the project began way back at that first spark, something mysteriously wonderful started to happen. It goes way beyond paper and canvas and clay and cardboard; even beyond walls and wood and steel and concrete. Perhaps it is that which created the spark to begin with, and remained true to its very essence all along. And just like that spark, we can't tell you exactly when, how, or why it happens. But we can tell you exactly what it is: It's Disney magic, pure and simple.

It is ageless and knows no bounds. The magic is that feeling when you are only nine and you get to drive a real car all by yourself, and when you are only ninety and a peek inside a turn-of-the-century firehouse makes you feel like you are nine again. It is that sudden lump in your throat when Mark Twain and Ben Franklin stand proudly before you—in person—on the torch of America's most beloved statue to reflect upon the meaning of its light. It is the reason that, when on the continent that for centuries has been home to the world's most fairytale-like castles, you single out its newest as the most fairytale-like castle in the world.

If you are truly into a Disney story, be it film or a three-dimensional world, you can feel the magic swell up within you. Gently, it captures your emotions, evokes a happy thought, brings back the child in you, and awakens a precious memory. There it suddenly appears, causing you to forget all your worldly cares, if even for a lovely moment or two. We may provide the stimulus, but certainly not the reaction. We make the magic real, but the real magic comes from inside you. Strange, but in all our creating, that which we do not actually create—but rather, you do—is our most treasured product.

Carrying on in the tradition born of the classic Disney films, the wonder and magic of storytelling continues today in Disney lands. This is what we, at Walt Disney Imagineering, are all about.

From the first spark that made it a dream, to the fantasy of believing that someday the dream might come true, through all the blood, sweat, and tears it took to make it real, to becoming part of that unmistakable Disney magic, the idea will live happily ever after.

The end.

Now, what if . . .

ABOVE: Every kingdom has its castle, and the "Vacation Kingdom of the World," the Walt Disney World Resort, is home to the majestic Cinderella Castle.

BOTTOM: One of the most recognized and beloved structures in the world, Sleeping Beauty Castle has welcomed hundreds of millions of guests into a kingdom of fantasy. What became the symbol of Disneyland at one time stood as the symbol of things to come. Walt could have chosen to build one of the castles from the animated classics *Snow White* or *Cinderella*, but he chose to introduce this one in 1955 to promote his most ambitious animated film project yet, scheduled for theatrical release four years later—*Sleeping Beauty*.

BELOW: Le Chateau de la Belle au Bois Dormant marks the entrance to Fantasyland at Disneyland Paris.

THE MAGIC OF DISNEYLAND

RIGHT: Walt Disney is clearly enchanted with his fine feathered friend, Jose, star of The Enchanted Tiki Room, the first fully-automated theatrical show. When the birds sang words and the flowers crooned together for the first time in 1963, the milestone event marked the public debut of Audio-Animatronics.

BELOW: On July 17, 1955, Disneyland welcomed its first guests. At the time, many of Walt Disney's entertainment industry peers thought he was crazy to attempt such a fantastic venture. Renowned architects excused the park's buildings as nothing more than cheap movie facades. Critics said Disneyland would not last more than six weeks. But proving to be more powerful than even the strongest criticism was the magic that was born that day. This magic proved to be so powerful, in fact, that it would soon grow to embrace the whole world.

LEFT: Many of Disneyland's attractions were based on a Disney film project. Inspired by Walt Disney's True-Life Adventure films, the Mine Train through Nature's Wonderland was no exception. The excursion featured over 200 fabricated animals, the thundering waterfalls of Cascade Peak, "Old Unfaithful" geyser and the colorful phosphorescent waterfalls inside the Rainbow Caverns.

LEFT BELOW: The spark for Disneyland was ignited as Walt watched his daughters enjoying themselves on a carousel in a west Los Angeles amusement park. Perhaps this is why, when his dream for a unique family park was coming true, King Arthur's Carrousel was included as the centerpiece of Fantasyland.

BELOW: The "Royal Street Bachelors" whip up a little New Orleans jazz in this French Quarter-inspired section of "town." New Orleans Square opened in 1966.

BOTTOM: Harry Anderson, Jr. and Michael Eisner join Mayor Mickey Mouse and his Disney character pals at the January 1993 gala grand opening ceremony of Mickey's Toontown. The Disneyland band was also on hand to keep everyone in "toon."

The Magic of The Magic Kingdom

WALT DISNEY WORLD
is a tribute to the philosophy and life of
Walter Elias Disney
...and to the talents, the dedication, and the loyalty
of the entire Disney organization that made Walt
Disney's dream come true. May Walt Disney World
bring Joy and Inspiration and New Knowledge to all
who come to this happy place... a Magic Kingdom
where the young at heart of all ages can laugh and
play and learn — together.

Dedicated this 25th day of October, 1971

Roy O. Disney

ABOVE: An estimated 52,000,000 people across the United States were introduced to Walt Disney World during a 90-minute NBC Television special that aired on October 29, 1971.

LEFT: After more than seven years of master planning, including 52 months of actual construction, the Walt Disney World Magic Kingdom opened on October 1, 1971. More than 8,000,000 cubic yards of earth were moved to accommodate the project. "Perhaps the biggest earth-moving operation since Hoover Dam," according to Look Magazine. Certainly it was America's largest private construction project. But Phase One, which included the Magic Kingdom and its neighboring resort facilities, encompassed only 2,500 of the more than 28,000 Disney acres (43 square miles), an area twice the size of Manhattan Island.

"You don't build it for yourself. You know what the people want and you build it for them."

—WALT DISNEY

ABOVE: With each term of office, the new President of the United States is added to the Hall of Presidents. The show presents a gathering of lifelike Audio-Animatronics figures representing every American President. Their spirited discussion culminates in a moving speech delivered by one of America's greatest orators, Abraham Lincoln.

BELOW: The new Tomorrowland, opened in February 1995, was inspired by the optimistic machine age of the 1930s, early publications of Mechanix Illustrated and Amazing Stories, and the future fantasies portrayed by Jules Verne and H.G. Wells. Now inhabited by robots, outer space aliens and, of course, a few humans, Tomorrowland is a place where everyday living is made better through science, invention and intergalactic influence. The future that never was is finally here!

ABOVE RIGHT: Each of the twelve 61-foot-long, 58-ton submarines—patterned after Captain Nemo's *Nautilus* from the Disney film *20,000 Leagues Under the Sea*—carries 38 passengers. The subs negotiate the incredible underwater world of the Fantasyland Lagoon to view lost continents and undersea wonders.

RIGHT: Splash Mountain made such a splash at Disneyland that development immediately began on this version for the Magic Kingdom at the Walt Disney World Resort. It opened in Florida in 1992.

The Magic of Epcot Future World

LEFT: Encompassing six acres, The Land pavilion explores the partnership between humans and the Earth on which they live. The Environmental Research Laboratory at the University of Arizona assisted Imagineering in establishing areas within this pavilion that, by using advanced agricultural methods such as hydroponics, grow vegetables served at its centrally located dining area.

BELOW: In cooperation with some of the most distinguished scientists and oceanographic experts in the world, Imagineering designed the largest facility ever dedicated to man's relationship with the ocean. As Michael Eisner began the January 1986 grand opening celebration, diver Mickey Mouse joined diver Frank Wells in the 5.7 million gallon seawater tank to help cut the ribbon. This event marked the first time Michael Eisner and Frank Wells, as The Walt Disney Company Chairman and CEO and President, respectively, appeared in the public eye to open an Imagineering project. And true to form, Frank really made a splash.

BOTTOM: Completely enclosed within a giant dome structure, the colorful Wonders of Life promotes and celebrates a healthy lifestyle with its health-minded attractions, shows, hands-on exhibits and dining facilities. This pavilion is home to the popular Cranium Command show.

Perhaps that which guided our dream to this destination was the flicker of magic itself. With a wick dipped in goodness, holding a flame as warm as the heart, its glow was powerful enough to brighten our darkest challenge and light the way.

LEFT: 80,000 photovoltaic cells cover The Universe of Energy, converting solar energy to electrical current to power the giant ride vehicles inside, which measure 18 feet wide by 29 feet long and can carry 97 passengers. These "traveling theater cars" ride on "sunshine" through two massive theaters and past dinosaurs in a primeval diorama that teaches guests about the origins and future of energy.

RIGHT: The Test Track presents guests with a thrilling opportunity usually reserved for highly skilled test drivers. Here, they get to feel what it is like to take a test car out on the multiple rigors and high speeds of an automotive proving ground test track. On a ride track that is over one mile in total length, this attraction is host to the longest and fastest ride system Imagineering has created to date. In one year, the combined fleet of "test vehicles" at this one location will travel over two million miles!

LEFT: Home to the delightful characters Dreamfinder and Figment, Journey Into Imagination offers a colorful, musical trip through the creative realm of the imagination process. The whimsical journey, found beneath the giant crystal-like pyramids of the pavilion, celebrates art, literature, and the performing arts and sciences.

BELOW: Appropriately situated in the heart of Future World, Innoventions brings Epcot guests an ever-changing kaleidoscope of consumer product technology. Inside, guests can get their hands on products—including prototypes—that are not yet available or have only recently become available in the marketplace. Providing major corporations the ongoing opportunity to showcase their "near future" products, Innoventions is one attraction that will never be finished.

The Magic of Epcot World Showcase

ABOVE: Every month is October at the Oktoberfest Musikanten in the Germany pavilion Biergarten. Although it is completely indoors, the restaurant appears to be the outside courtyard of a picturesque sixteenth-century German town. Nightly celebrations feature the finest German beers and oompah bands.

LEFT: The China pavilion at Epcot features an elaborate structure styled after the Temple of Heaven in Beijing. In order to faithfully depict the intricate tilework patterns of the original, Imagin-eering artisans screenprinted hundreds of exact replications of its detailed patterns onto each and every tile at Epcot. Even from a short distance away, a guest might recognize the tiles as authentic.

BELOW LEFT: The authentic avenues of the Morocco pavilion appear as though they have been in existence for centuries. Guests often comment that once they step away from the World Showcase Promenade and disappear into the hidden back-streets of Morocco, they feel as though they are not at Epcot at all.

BELOW: Inside the Mexico pavilion at World Showcase, the fountain of Fuente del Chorrito graces the Plaza de los Amigos, a town square styled in the architecture of Taxco.

ABOVE: The centerpiece of World Showcase is the American Adventure. The pavilion's 1,024-seat theater presents a fully automated stage and film show, unlike any in the world, about America's greatest struggles and triumphs. The show features several innovative technologies, including massive automated sets that are moved into position on railroad-like tracks and the first "walking" Audio-Animatronics figure in the form of Benjamin Franklin.

TOP: Entrance into the Italy pavilion is marked by two pillars graced with the statues of St. Theodore and the Dragon and the Lion of St. Marks. A replica of the fourteenth-century Doge's Palace in Venice lies on the left, flanked by the 100-foot-high landmark bell tower, the Campanile.

RIGHT: Situated on the World Showcase Promenade, a replica of the eighth-century pagoda at Horyuji in Nara gracefully announces the serene realm of the Japan pavilion. Eighty-three feet in height, the goju-no-to, or pagoda, features five levels that represent the elements from which Buddhists believe all things are created: earth, water, fire, wind, and sky.

The Magic of Tokyo Disneyland

ABOVE: Tokyo Disneyland draws much of its success from the fact that many Japanese guests are not only big Disney fans, but they enjoy American culture as well. The Mark Twain Riverboat and the Tom Sawyer Island rafts bring living stories of America to the park.

ABOVE RIGHT: Dumbo not only flies, but he breaks the language barrier while giving Tokyo Disneyland guests a lift in Fantasyland.

BELOW: The most recognizable face in the world blossoms into a smile at the entrance to Tokyo Disneyland, the first Disney theme park constructed outside of the United States. Note the enormous glass-enclosed structure above the main entrance which, in anticipation of inclement weather, was built to enclose the World Bazaar.

The magic of what we have created is the emotion of music, the vibration of color, the sensation of light, the absence of time. It is a window to what was, and a doorway to what will be. The magic is a cherished moment remembered for a lifetime.

ABOVE: Even though snow is infrequent in Tokyo, the city still gets its share on occasion. No matter what the weather, Tokyo Disneyland guests can always enjoy a stroll along the World Bazaar, this park's version of Main Street.

LEFT ABOVE: Following in the tradition of their wise-cracking counterparts in the USA, the Jungle Cruise Skippers at Tokyo Disneyland deliver jokes that are just as corny in Japanese as they are in English.

LEFT BELOW: Takahashi-san, then President of the Oriental Land Company, joins Card Walker, then Chairman of Walt Disney Productions, to help some friends dedicate Disney's first international theme park venture.

ABOVE: Just beyond Hollywood Boulevard at Lakeside Circle is Echo Lake, home to Min and Bill's Dockside Diner and Dinosaur Gertie's Ice Cream of Extinction.

RIGHT: In a spectacular gala event, all the glitter and glamour of "tinseltown" came out to shine with some of the biggest stars in Hollywood for the grand opening celebration at the Disney-MGM Studios.

RIGHT BELOW: From westerns to movie musicals to every film genre in between, The Great Movie Ride puts you right in the middle of the action. In this scene, a gangster is about to make his getaway in a vehicle full of guests!

ABOVE: One of the greatest achievements of our engineers and special effects illusioneers actually turned out to be a real catastrophe—Catastrophe Canyon, that is. A major earthquake unleashes fire, explosions, a full-sized tanker truck, and a 70,000 gallon flood on a backstage full of guests—every four minutes!

BELOW LEFT: Bringing together architectural styles from the heyday of Hollywood in the '30s and '40s, Sunset Boulevard paves the way to a wondrous land whose boundaries are those of the imagination. That's the signpost up ahead—your next stop is Twilight Zone Tower of Terror.

The Magic of Disneyland Paris

ABOVE: The Disneyland Hotel stands at the entrance to Disneyland Paris, providing guests with a spectacular view of the park. From the windows of the hotel, the magic of Disneyland is the last thing the guests see at night and the first thing they see in the morning.

BELOW: After the Pirate Ship and landmark Skull Rock were removed from Disneyland, Captain Hook proved he was no chicken of the sea by setting sail for France and dropping anchor near Adventure Isle.

ABOVE: Europe's best-loved tales inspired some of Walt Disney's finest moments in storytelling. The favor was returned to this land when on April 12, 1992, only four years after Imagineering completed design plans, Disneyland Paris was dedicated in Marne-la-Vallée, France.

RIGHT: At the highest point of Adventure Isle, La Cabane des Robinson—that's the "Swiss Family Treehouse"—awaits exploration and adventure.

BELOW: This turn-of-the-century Main Street cop at Disneyland Paris responds with a smile as this little English-speaking guest repeats what he thinks is, "oui oui!"

BOTTOM: The design of Discoveryland pays tribute to some of the great visionaries of Europe, including Jules Verne, H.G. Wells, and Leonardo da Vinci. In the background, the nose of the great Victorian airship Hyperion can be seen poking out from under the eaves of Videopolis, the largest food and entertainment complex at Disneyland Paris. The Orbitron (in right foreground) was styled after the eighteenth- and nineteenth-century planetary sculptures that can be seen in museums throughout Europe.

The Magic of The Walt Disney World Resort

BELOW: The Polynesian Village resort hotel is designed in a relaxing South Seas style. Its Great Ceremonial House sits on the white sand beachfront of the Seven Seas Lagoon, a 200-acre lagoon man-made for sailing, swimming, and special nighttime water shows.

RIGHT: One of the first of two hotels constructed at Walt Disney World (the other being the Polynesian Resort), the Contemporary showcased a bold new technological innovation in steel-framed unitized or modular construction. Each of the 1,500 steel-framed rooms and baths (including electrical, plumbing, and fixtures) was completely prefabricated and delivered by truck to the A-frame structure, then lifted into position by a giant crane.

RIGHT BELOW: The rustic Pioneer Hall at Fort Wilderness Campground is the home of the ever-popular Hoop-Dee-Doo Musical Revue. The singin' and dancin' Pioneer Hall Players rustle up a rousing dinner show here every night in grand western style.

LEFT: Covering 56 acres, Typhoon Lagoon features the largest inland surfing lagoon in the world. Twice the size of a football field, the lagoon generates the world's largest artificially created waves—up to $6\frac{1}{2}$ feet high. Blown here by the "storm," the fishing boat "Miss Tilly" balances precariously on top of the 95-foot-high Mt. Mayday.

ABOVE: Opened in 1989 at Walt Disney World Village, Pleasure Island is a revolutionary concept in Imagineering-designed nighttime entertainment. The design team traveled the world to research all kinds of night clubs while creating the story and theme for the island. The "abandoned waterfront district" features unique night-clubs, restaurants and shops—highlighted by Planet Hollywood and a multi-screen theater complex.

LEFT: A ski resort was built here after a freak blizzard dumped mountains of snow in central Florida. Melting snow turned ski runs into water slides. On April 1, 1995, the 66-acre Blizzard Beach officially became a water wonder-land! At 120 feet high, Summit Plummet "ski jump" is the highest, fastest water slide in the world—reaching speeds up to 55 mph!

LEFT: Imagineering designed the displays, galleries and organizing themes for the Autry Museum of Western Heritage in Griffith Park in Los Angeles. This chuckwagon exhibit is part of the "Cowboy Gallery."

BELOW: Giant lava lights welcome guests to a science fiction–themed restaurant proposed for the Los Angeles International Airport, in this concept sketch by Gil Keppler.

ABOVE: To support Walt Disney's involvement as Pageantry Committee Chairman for the 1960 VIII Winter Olympic Games at Squaw Valley near Lake Tahoe, California, Imagineering Senior Vice President John Hench designed the "Tower of Nations" for the opening and closing ceremonies. The ceremonial staging area included two massive 24-foot-high snow sculptures depicting a male and female athlete. This marked the first time snow sculptures had ever been used for a Winter Olympics. The completed design included thirty flagpoles for each of the competing nations, as well as other snow statues featuring athletes in action.

The magic is as wide as a smile and as narrow as a wink, loud as laughter and quiet as a tear, tall as a tale and deep as emotion. So strong, it can lift the spirit. So gentle, it can touch the heart. It is the magic that begins the happily ever after.

TOP LEFT: The premiere of Disney's version of virtual reality, called the Aladdin Magic Carpet Adventure, was put to the test in Walt Disney Imagineering Labs at Epcot in 1994. Using the characters and styling from the film *Aladdin*, the interactive experience delivered "a whole new world" of entertainment.

ABOVE: Phillip Freer's concept rendering of the Aladdin Magic Carpet Adventure suggests how the hardware for the virtual reality experience might be staged for use by Epcot guests.

TOP RIGHT: When Walt Disney World requested an 18-hole miniature golf course, Joe Lanzisero, an Imagineer who had always dreamed of designing such a project, jumped on the idea. Of the four different concepts he designed for the course, "Fantasia Gardens" was selected since its theme was most compatible with the proposed site—in front of the landmark Swan and Dolphin Hotels.

RIGHT: Working with The Disney Store, Imagineering designed the Roman-themed Disney Store at Caesar's Forum Mall in Las Vegas. Two more themed stores have since been added in San Francisco and New York City.

BACKGROUND: Introducing a new era in Imagineering design "outside the berm," the Walt Disney Gallery made its debut at the Main Place Mall in Santa Ana, California. Operated by The Disney Store, the Gallery offers merchandise in a whimsical "cartoon-nouveau" environment.

Why we do what we do

ABOVE: To commemorate the opening of Epcot on October 1, 1982, the Imagineers created a giant edible model of the project—Epcake, the Experimental Prototype Cake of Tomorrow!

FAR RIGHT: At the same time guests were taking the opening-day plunge down Splash Mountain at Walt Disney World, Imagineers were plunging into the "Splash Bash" being held back home to celebrate the completion of the attraction. Here, Jim Armstrong, Ru Chao, Mike Gordon and Anton Burrell are keeping a log on the festivities.

THIS PAGE AND OPPOSITE: Buttons, buttons—have we got the buttons! Whenever Imagineering completes a project, there is usually a button or other such item distributed to help us commemorate the event. (Sorry, not available in any store. Supplies are limited—to us!)

People often ask us, "why do you do what you do?" There are probably as many answers to that question as there are Imagineers. But we all agree one of the biggest reasons we do it is for the excitement that comes with opening day!

Our mission is to create fun and imaginative experiences that make people happy. In that sense, our quintessential product is a smile. A smile is a magical thing. Creating that very special kind of magic is truly the greatest "job" in the world.

We work in an environment that encourages us to create and to have fun while we do it. That is not to say we don't work hard. But in the captivating spirit of teamwork, the challenge of inventing and the pure joy of creating, oftentimes we don't even notice the hard work. Many people out in the workaday world ask, "is it Friday yet?" Many Imagineers ask, "is it Friday already?"

By dreaming and nurturing and building the things we do, we add to the magic in the Disney parks. At the same time, we add to the magic of our own lives.

Why do we do what we do?

Because at Imagineering, we never know what to expect from each new day, or from ourselves, especially knowing that excellence is always within our reach.

Because we just can't wait to see the future.

Because we can build a stagecoach, a space ship, a rock & roll performing robot, an erupting volcano, a storyboard, a computer model, a computer, a talking drinking fountain, a prototype camera and projector, a digital soundtrack and a stage set, all in the same place on the same day.

We do it because we are interested in how things work and in making things work.

Because we are artists passionate about science, and scientists passionate about the arts.

Because, unlike creating a film or television show that is released for a brief period of time, our creations are designed to provide continuous enjoyment for many years to come.

We do it so children can learn without even realizing they are learning.

For grownups, who are just children all grown up.

For Walt.

For each other.

We do it because we believe in the family.

Because our parks are

"We're just getting started, so if any of you starts to rest on your laurels, just forget it."

—WALT DISNEY

ABOVE: After designer Don Carson wrapped-up his concept-to-completion effort at Mickey's Toontown at Disneyland, he put his "Murphy" character to work to explain the entire Imagineering process in a single cartoon.

FAR LEFT: The day Typhoon Lagoon took Walt Disney World by storm, Imagineers like Chick Russell, along with his wife Jaye and sons Charlie and William, blew ashore to the "Typhoon Party" in Los Angeles to help ring in the event.

among the few things in this world that people of all ages, races, creeds, convictions, languages and physical capabilities can all enjoy at the same time together. We do what we do, most of all, for them.

Like the young widow from Ohio, who is working very hard and doing without the things she needs for herself, so she can take her two children to Walt Disney World.

Like the people who gather around the World Showcase Lagoon at Epcot and cheer like crazy after the finale of our nighttime show Illuminations—even in the pouring rain.

Like the young boy who is literally spinning like a top with excitement as he waits in line for Splash Mountain after its grand opening shouting, "It's open! It's open! It's open!"

Like the president of a giant European corporation, who, while riding Space Mountain in Disneyland Paris, holds tightly onto his head so he doesn't lose his hat—his Goofy hat.

Like the dad who suddenly catches himself whistling "It's a Small World After All" while driving his family back home to Omaha.

Like the college student who, while visiting Wonders of Life at Epcot, experiences something that suddenly sparks in her an interest in the field of medicine.

Like the young girl who can't stop laughing because a giant dog sneezed real sneeze all over her glasses in Honey, I Shrunk the Audience.

Like the Viet Nam Vet who sheds a silent tear of pride and remembrance in the American Adventure at Epcot.

Like the grandma who is sitting on a bench tenderly humming the melody to "Baby Mine" to her baby granddaughter after allowing the bigger kids to go on Dumbo all by themselves.

We do it for the terminally ill little boy whose greatest wish is to come to Disneyland. For the mounting anticipation he feels weeks, then days, then hours, then minutes before he enters the front gate. For the moment he makes that transition from his world into the Happiest Place on Earth. For his first big smile inside the park, and for the magical smile that comes as he lies in bed late that night, closing his eyes and thinking about nothing else but all the wonderful things he did and saw that day.

For that smile.

OVERLEAF: You would think that after having just completed Epcot, the largest private construction project in the world, we could have found a ladder tall enough to properly take this picture so you would know we are not just standing around in a big group releasing balloons to celebrate its October 1, 1982 grand opening. We are actually assembled together to form the words: "WE DID IT!"

The magic rejuvenates the body, stimulates the mind and inspires the spirit. It is a source of happiness and a fountain of learning. The magic is also that feeling of anticipation when something wonderful is about to happen, and the joyous fulfillment of expectation when it does.

The magic is that feeling when dreams come true.
The magic is real, and its spark lives in you!

IT ALL STARTED WITH A MOUSE

Mickey Mouse, as the Sorcerer's Apprentice, conjures up a fitting logo for Walt Disney Imagineering. In a scene from *Fantasia*, the Sorcerer's Apprentice somehow manages to make magical things happen without expecting them to. We owe Mickey a great deal of gratitude. If it were not for him, there probably would not be an Imagineering.

Sure, the mild-mannered little mouse is an all-around good guy, a character who represents Everyman. But he is also our hero. When Mickey appeared on the scene in 1928, he actually represented salvation for Walt and Roy Disney at a time when things were not going well in their business. In fact, Mickey was born on the train ride back to California from New York after Walt received devastating financial news that impacted his then-current production projects. When he returned to Hollywood, he did not come back empty-handed.

"Born out of necessity," Walt Disney fondly recalled about his best friend, "the little fellow literally freed us of immediate worry. He provided the means for expanding our organization to its present dimensions and for extending the medium of cartoon animation towards new entertainment levels."

But Mickey provided much more than that. He lent us a hand in giving all our parks a most magical character.

ABOVE LEFT: John Hench, the "official portrait artist" of Mickey Mouse, captured our hero as he appeared on his 50th birthday, showing off an early concept of Epcot.

ABOVE MIDDLE: The fountain at Mickey's Toontown in Disneyland flows with pride for its most outstanding citizen.

ABOVE RIGHT: Mickey is on top of the world at the Disney-MGM Studios.

BACKGROUND: One of the many faces of Mickey blossoms at the main entrance of Disneyland.

OPPOSITE: Walt Disney had an uncanny ability to recognize hidden talents in individuals who may not have been aware they had them. One day in 1954, Walt mentioned to special effects film animator Blaine Gibson that he wanted him to sculpt a few projects for Disneyland. This took Blaine completely by surprise, especially since his only attempt at "sculpting" was carving bars of soap just for fun. But he soon embarked on a legendary career that carried him though more than three decades of sculpting the majority of classic Disney theme park characters, from ghosts to bears, pirates to presidents. Blaine came out of retirement to sculpt this larger-than-life bronze statue, titled "Partners," which was unveiled in the central plaza at Disneyland on Mickey's birthday in November, 1993. It seems fitting that Blaine's finest work honors the man who somehow knew he had the talent to do such things.

"I only hope that we never lose sight of one thing—that it was all started by a mouse."

—WALT DISNEY

There are two ways to look at this blank sheet of paper. You can look at it as the last page of a book, or as the greatest opportunity in the world because nobody's put anything on it. That's the way we look at it at Imagineering. Go ahead and use it to dream, create new things and let your imagination go.

Why not? Everything begins somewhere . . .